RATE P

A LIST OF EMIGRANTS FROM ENGLAND TO AMERICA, 1682-1692

A LIST OF EMIGRANTS
FROM ENGLAND TO AMERICA
1682–1692

Transcribed from the original records at the
City of London Record Office
by

MICHAEL GHIRELLI, B.A.

by courtesy of the Corporation of London

With Introductory Notes by Marion J. Kaminkow

Magna Carta Book Company
Baltimore 15, Maryland
1968

CONTENTS

INTRODUCTORY NOTES

This list of names of early emigrants to the American and West Indian Colonies is now published for the first time, although the existence of the manuscript has been known for some years. The names have been extracted from a series of manuscript volumes in the Record Office of the City of London, known as the *Lord Mayor's Waiting Books*. Like so many other names of the colonial period, they are mostly, but not all, those of young people who wished to emigrate to the colonies but who lacked the means to pay their passage; so they bound themselves to serve for a specified number of years without pay in return for their passage across the ocean and certain emoluments at the end of their service. In some cases the employer of the servant engaged him personally or through agents in England, but in most cases the servants were shipped out by sea captains or agents who collected their fee from the employer in the colonies; in other words, the servants were sold.

Many thousands of men and women, not all of them destitute, as can be deduced from the trades which many of them followed, took advantage of the custom of indentured servitude, as it was called, to transport themselves to a new way of life in the American colonies. Many suffered great hardships but most endured their servitude and reaped certain rewards at the end of their time in the form of land, seed and tools, with which to become planters in their turn, if they so desired. Later, many of them bought servants and became prosperous and nearly all of them became the progenitors of families which now populate all parts of the United States. Some of them rose to eminence and took part in government; it is known that seven burgesses of an early Virginia Assembly were former servants and that Benjamin Franklin's maternal grandmother was also a servant. Very few of the servants kept diaries telling us exactly how they fared, but the diary of John Harrower and two letters from servants are listed in the bibliography.

Certain individuals are entered in the *Waiting Books* as having received a pass from the Lord Mayor of London, to travel, which seems to have been necessary at certain times, and they presumably paid their own fares; and while this may indicate that they were from a more prosperous class, they have left us far fewer facts about themselves. Only their names and destinations have been entered, with the date on which the pass was issued.

The *Lord Mayor's Waiting Books* are twenty one large tomes wherein are

entered the daily happenings in the Lord Mayor's Court.   Volumes 13 and 14
are the only ones which cover the years wherein official registration of servants was required but a number of passes to travel occur in volume 15.
There are a few paying passengers in volumes 13 and 14 also, and two parties
of French Huguenots who are included here with the rest (See FLEURRIOTT,
ANBIER and REYNAULT).

When this list is compared with similar lists of names of indentured servants emigrating from the British Isles to the American Plantations,   it will
be be noted at once that the dates tend to correspond. The records of Middlesex, extracted from the records at the Middlesex Guildhall and published by
C. D. P. Nicholson in the *Genealogist' Magazine,*   1955-8, cover the years
1683-4; and those from Bristol, published in 1929 under the title *Bristol and
America* are for the years 1654-85.   The Bristol records prove that indentured
servitude was already a well-established custom before the present list was
originally made;   in fact it was established by the Virginia Company at a
very early date.

The published records of the State Papers and Privy Council Registers
reveal that these names were collected during one of the periods of government intervention in the registration of indentured servants, when officials
were required to oversee the procedure in order to prevent foul play.   Pre-
viously, on Sept. 7, 1664, Roger Whitley had been appointed by Parliament
as master of the office for registering servants in London, at a salary of forty
shillings per year and such allowances as the planters agreed; but in 1682
the Privy Council decided that Roger Whitley's office was failing to do its
job properly.   It was reported that there were numerous cases of agents
stealing away people for the plantations, a practice known as "spiriting",
or inveigling people under false pretenses.   The Privy Council therefore
decreed that prospective servants must be bound in the presence of a justice
of the peace or the mayor or chief magistrate.   This is the decree which
brought about the present list of names by requiring them to be registered in
the Mayor's Court Records, and it is printed in full at the end of the book as
Appendix II.

It was probably in 1686 that registration of indentured servants once again
reverted to semi-private hands, for there are no more servants entered in this
list after that date.   Those few names for the later years are of private
persons applying for passes to travel, mostly in the year 1690, tapering off
to 8 in 1691 and only 1 in 1692.   Mention is made in the Privy Council
records of Messrs. Legge and Guise being in charge of the office for registering servants and in May 1689 the appointment was given to Edward Thompson
who was appointed for twenty one years at a fee of five shillings for every
indenture and sixpence for registering each name. *(Acts of the Privy Council,
Colonial, volume II p. 128).*   No extensive list of emigrants from the period

when registration was in semi-private hands has ever been found.

Registration became a government concern once again in 1717 when the Felons' Act was passed, containing a clause requiring servants to register before the Lord Mayor of London. The framers were probably ignorant of the Thompson office and were concerned that young people who wished to emigrate might become petty thieves in order to secure transportation for themselves at government expense. (See Kaminkow's *Original Lists of Emigrants in Bondage,* where this Act is printed in full). A petition appeared before Parliament soon afterwards from Leonard Thompson of Gray's Inn (probably the son of Edward Thompson who had inherited the business), stating that "The late King William did grant to your petitioner letters patent for the sole registering of all such servants, male and female that should voluntarily go or be sent to any of His Majesty's Plantations in America or elsewhere... that there is the merchants' clause in the said act which affects your petitioner's property..."

It was recommended that his petition be heard before a committee, but it was evidently dismissed because in 1718 the indentures begin to be registered once more before the mayor or justice of the peace of London. These later names have already been printed in Kaminkow's *A List of Emigrants from England to America, 1718-1759.* These were transcribed from the individual indentures issued at that time and now kept in boxes at the City of London Record Office. As far as is known, very few indentures for these later dates have come to light from any other ports.

Very little is known definitely about the practice of "spiriting", apart from the numerous rumors and literary anecdotes such as those in Defoe's *Colonel Jack* and *Memoirs of an Unfortunate Young Nobleman.* (See bibliography). That the rumors were not idle is proved by various cases which came up in the Lord Mayor's Court and are duly recorded in the Waiting Books. There are a number of warrants granted by the Lord Mayor for fetching back individuals who had been illegally inveigled aboard ship but no prosecutions seem to have taken place; it is merely decreed that the individual shall be brought back without charge by a certain date, if already departed, or taken off the ship if it had not already sailed. In one case a bond was to be posted for the servant's safe return and a sum of money given to her upon her arrival home. The injustice is apparent when we consider the dire punishments meted out to those who stole a paltry sum of money or object, when compared with the lack of punishment inflicted upon a merchant or sea captain who stole away a human being. The cases are printed in the appendix and further instances are to be found printed in volume 4 of Stock's *Proceedings and Debates of British Parliaments Respecting North America.*

The entries in the Lord Mayor's Waiting Books are written in six or more different hands in rotation, their styles of writing appearing regularly every six weeks or so.   The relevant entries, often entered among different pieces of business, read similar to the following; "2 Oct. 1684. Martin Franklyn son of Richard Franklyn late of Kilburne, Middlesex, husbandman, bound to Peter Barton to serve in Virginia for four years".   In the margin is the note: "Franklyn bound to Barton".   Unlike the later indentures, the names of the persons to whom the servant was bound do not appear with great frequency, each employer appearing to be content with one or two servants.   Agents of the later period collected whole shiploads of servants and sent them over as a cargo to be sold but that stage had not perhaps been reached in London as yet.   It is believed that in many cases the name is that of the actual master whom the servant was to work for, and not an agent who undertook to transport and sell the servant.   However, since this can not be discovered with certainty, they are referred to as agents.   In some cases, owing to the several different handwritings, there are seeming discrepancies in the spelling of the names so that it is not always possible to tell whether the same or a different agent is meant;   for instance, one wonders whether John Dykes is the same as John Dix and whether Philip Gower, Philip Gowre and Philip Gore are all the same person.

The entries are not consistent in that sometimes the place of origin and age are given, and sometimes they are not.   In many cases, there are witnesses to the registration who testify that the servant was not already an apprentice, that he had no dependents and that he had parental permission to emigrate if under age.   The witnesses were supposed to be familiar with the servant and often they were relatives or old friends; but occasionally we find the same person acting for several separate persons and some occur in other circumstances as agents, or servants themselves and some may have been relatives or friends of the agents.   Some of the servants are mere children of ten or twelve, and the act of 1717 recognised this sad fact and tried to put a stop to it by stating that none were to be registered under the age of fifteen.

A unique feature of this list is the frequent listing of a parent's name, usually with his trade and place of origin, even though, in the large majority of cases the father is dead, the entry reading deced. (deceased).   In many cases also, the mother has re-married or reverted to her maiden name, for there are endless discrepancies between the names of the parents and the children.   A step father is invariably described as a father-in-law.

The place names often give difficulties, but they have been transcribed exactly as they are spelled, often by clerks who were quite unfamiliar with the geography of the British Isles.   Where the name of the place is not clear, it has been followed in parenthesis by what is probably meant.   Although not all give the names of their places of origin, it is clear that the emigrants came from all over the British Isles from as far apart as Devonshire and the

Isles of Orkney.

Another interesting side light is the gathering by the Pensilvania Society in Philadelphia of glass bottle makers. Joseph Martin appears to have been the London agent for this company, and glass bottle makers seem to have been sought for by him to work for the company.

In transcribing these records, all spelling has been modernised, except the names of places, as described above, and any direct quotations; but the abbreviations in direct quotes have been given in full, for the sake of clarity, except the word deceased, which always appears as in the original "deced".

M. J. Kaminkow
1968

ANALYSIS OF SEX AND DESTINATIONS

Males: 670
Females: 290

Destinations

America	2
Antego or Antigua	9
Barbadoes	125
Barbadoes and Antigua	1
Boston	4
Carolina	15
East New Jersey	1
Jamaica	321
Maryland	182
Maryland and New Jersey	1
Maryland in Virginia	1
Montserrat	9
Nevis	15
New England	10
New Providence	5
New York	8
North Carolina	1
Pensylvania	23
Pennsylvania (Philadelphia)	1
Pennsylvania or West Jersey	4
Port Royal, Jamaica	3
St. Christophers	3
Tobago	1
Virginia	205
West Indies	4
No destination given	6

These figures are approximate

BIBLIOGRAPHY

English Historical Documents. Ed. David D. Douglas. Volume IX - American Colonial Documents to 1776. (Contains two letters from servants in 1756; Elizabeth Sprigs and Thomas Lloyd).

Proceedings and Debates of British Parliaments Respecting North America, 1542-1783. Ed. L. F. Stock.

Acts of the Privy Council of England (Colonial Series). 6 volumes covering the years 1613-1783. 1909-12.

Smith, Abbot E. Indentured Servitude. In Journal of Economic History Volume II pp. 40-53. May 1942. (This deals largely with methods of recruiting servants and the spiriting problem).

Smith, Abbot E. Colonists in Bondage. 1947.

Ballage, James C. White Servitude in the Colony of Virginia. Johns Hopkins University Studies in Political Science, volume XIII. 1895.

Herrick, Cheesman A. White Servitude in Pennsylvania. 1926.

McCormick, Eugene I. White Servitude in Maryland. 1904.

Morris, Richard B. Government and Labor in Early America. 1946. Reprinted, 1965.

Eddis, William. Letters from America, Historical and Descriptive, comprising occurences from 1769-1777 inclusive. 1792.

Crevecoeur, J. Hector St. John. Letters from an American farmer. Many editions.

Alsop, George. A Character of the Province of Maryland, 1666. Several editions. (Alsop emigrated as a servant and after finishing his time returned to England. The picture he paints of his own servitude and the delights of the colony are very glowing and one suspects that he was engaged as a procurer of servants himself, after his return to England).

Kaminkow, Jack and Marion. A List of Emigrants from England to America, 1718-1759. 1966.

Kaminkow, Marion and Jack. Original Lists of Emigrants in Bondage from London to the American Colonies, 1719-1744. 1967.

Diary of John Harrower, 1773-6. In American Historical Review volume 6, pp. 65-107. (The only known diary of a servant. He was a schoolteacher who left his wife and children and sold himself for a servant for four years. He lived well on a plantation where he was employed as a schoolmaster, after having been well treated on the ship. He sent for his wife and children but the diary ends before we learn what happened).

Defoe, Daniel. The History and Remarkable Life of the Truly Honourable Col. Jaque, commonly called Jack...who was...six and twenty years a thief and then kidnapped to Virginia.

Defoe, Daniel. Moll Flanders.

Memoirs of an Unfortunate Young Nobleman Returned from 13 Years Slavery in America, where he had been sent by the Wicked Contrivances of his Cruel Uncle. Printed for J. Freeman, 1743. (This is supposed to have been founded on the true story of Lord Annesley's son who was disposed of by his uncle because he stood in his way as heir to the estate. The usual story of hardship in the colonies is enlivened by amorous adventures and he eventually returned safely home. This story also occurs in *State Trials* volume 17, p. 1139; Andrew Lang - *The Annesley Case,* 1913 and *Peregrine Pickle* by Smollett.)

LIST OF EMIGRANTS FROM ENGLAND TO AMERICA

The parentage, place of origin and age of each emigrant are only given where they were entered in the originals. Direct quotes are given in inverted commas and editorial notes in parenthesis. The record references at the end of each line refer to book and page numbers, where page numbers are available, since all the original pages are not numbered. The records from which the names are taken are described in the Introductory Notes.

ADAMS, William. Somersett. Bound to James Fawcett for 4 years in Maryland. 26 or thereabouts. Jan. 5, 1684. 14/113

ALLEN, Robert. Son of Thomas Allen of Citty of Worster, weaver, deced. Bound to David Lockwood for 4 years in Jamaica. Nov. 4, 1684. 14/49

ALLEN, Thomas. See BECKFORD, Peter.

ALLETT, Peter. Son of Thomas Allett of Over in Cheshire, weaver, deced. Bound to John West for 4 years in Jamaica. Age 30. Feb. 28, 1684 14/166

ALLIN, Richard. Son of Richard Allin late of the Citty of Oxford. Bound to David Greenhill for 4 years in Jamaica. March 17, 1684. 14/190

AMBROSE, Henry. Bound to Thomas Nicholls for 7 years in Pensilvania or West Jersey. Age 14. April 9, 1686. Witness Alice Paine. 14/559

AMES, Sarah. Daughter of Thomas Ames of Leather Land (Lane?) in St. Andrews, Holbourne, London, labourer. Bound to John Worthington of Maryland for 4 years. Sept. 11, 1684. 14/6

AMIES, Anthony.   Son of Lazarus Amies, scrivener.   Bound to Thomas
Tenche for 4 years in Maryland.   Aug. 13, 1684.   13

AMPS?, Thomas.   Bound to Charles Smith for 4 years in Jamaica.   Age 30.
Dec. 18, 1684.   14/99

ANBIER or AUBIER, BARON, BANCE,REYNAULT, (Henry, Elizabeth, Fancois
and Marie).   VIELLET, FLEURIOTT (Jean and Louise).   "These eleven
persons are French Protestants and were bound at the request of Mr. Jean du
Mastre and Mrs. Stephen Noguier (or Nognier), deacons of the French Church
in London".   14/353

ANBIER or AUBIER, Moyse or Meyse.   A Frenchman of London, mason.   Bound
to Marmaduke Larkin for 4 years in Jamaica. Aug. 3, 1685. See above. 14/353

ANDERHILL, George.   Printer.   Bound to Thomas Meache for 4 years in
New Yorke.   June 16, 1686.   Witness Barthew. Sprint, printer of Old Change.
(London).   14

ANDERSON, Andrew of Salkirke, Scotland.   Labourer.   Bound to Robert
Burman for 4 years in Maryland.   Age 21.   Aug. 5, 1685.   "This man is
a soldier discharged from the army".   14/355

ANDERSON, James.   Douglas, Clidesdaleshire (Probably Lanarkshire),
Scotland.   Labourer.   Bound to John Balson for 4 years in Jamaica. Nov.
26, 1684.   14/74

ANDREWES, George and Jane, his wife.   Bound to Samuell Pratt for 4 years
in Jamaica.   Dec. 17, 1684.   14/97

ANNISON, Edward of Hackney, Middlesex.   Bound to Richard Fyfe for 4
years in Maryland.   July 18, 1684.   13

ANSELL, Elizabeth, spinster.   Bound to Peter Febber for 4 years in Virginia.
Age. 17.   Sept. 23, 1685.   Witness Prudence Ansell of Mile End, Stepney,
(London), widow.   14/413

ANSLEY, Mathew.   Son of Mathew Ansley of Banbury in Oxon, linen draper,
deced.   Bound to Thomas Bannister for 8 years in New England.   May 13,
1685.   Witness Thomas Harcott, servt. to the Banbury carrier.   14/250

APPLETON, Nicholas.   Son of Ralph Appleton of Carne (Colne), Lancashire,
clothier, deced. Bound to John Moorhead for 4 years in Jamaica. May 8, 1685.
Witness John Okeley, St. Giles in the Fields (London or Middlesex).   14/243

ARKINSTALL, John.   Son of John Arkinstall of Wem, Sallopp (Shropshire), bodice maker, deced.   Bound to Charles Richards for 4 years in Jamaica. Age 22.   March 24, 1685.   14/549

ARMSTRONG, James.   "Upon affirmation of Elizabeth Armstrong, his sister, living in Castle Ally, Holbourne (London) that he was neither apprentice nor married.   Bound to Barnaby Cater for 4 years in Barbados.   April 28, 1685.   14/227

ARNOLD, Thomas.   Son of Jeremiah Arnold, St. Sepulchers, London, silversmith.   Bound to William Thorowgood for 5 years in Carolina.   Aug. 14, 1684.   13

ASHENDEN, Robert.   Son of Robert Ahsenden.   Bound to Crafurn Setter for 7 years in Carolina.   Feb. 7, 1682.   13

ASHLEY, Elizabeth.   Daughter of Richard Ashley of Whitelyon Street in St. Giles in the Fields, Middlesex, deced.   Bound to John Pelly for 4 years in Barbadoes.   April 4, 1685.   14/211

ASHLEY, Rebecka.   Daughter of Jeremiah Ashley late of Benfleet, Essex. Bound to Thomas Blake for 4 years in Barbados.   Age 20.   Unmarried. March 25, 1685.   14/195

ATKINS, Christian.   Daughter of Michaell Atkins late of Newcastle.   (No county, could be Northumberland or Staffordshire).   Bound to Phillip Gower for 4 years in Jamaica.   Unmarried.   March 25, 1685.   14/195

ATKINS, Edward.   Son of Thomas Atkins late of Wilden, Bedfordshire, shoemaker, deceased.   Bound to John Williams for 4 years in Barbadoes. Age 25.   April 24, 1685. (See Additions and Corrections).   14/222

ATKINS, John.   Son of Robert Atkins late of London, perriwigmaker, deced. Bound to Henerye Robinson for 10 years in Maryland.   Age 12.   Aug. 31, 1685.   Witness Elizabeth Robinson, his mother.   14/386

AUBIER.   See ANBIER.

AUNGIER, Samuel.   To Barbados.   Nov. 14, 1690.   15/122

AUSTIN, Elizabeth.   Spinster.   Bound to Anthony Cornwell for 4 years in Maryland.   Age 23.   Oct. 20, 1685.   14/435

3

AUSTIN, John.   Brother of Elizabeth above.   Bound to Anthony Cornwell for 4 years in Maryland.   Age 22.   Oct. 20, 1685.   14/435

AYRES, Elizabeth.   Daughter of Edward Ayres of Launceston, Cornwall "By consent of Elizabeth Volereen, her aunt".   Bound to Joseph Bartholomew for 4 years in Jamaica.   March 31, 1685.   14/205

AYRES, Thomas.   Son of Thomas Ayres of Drury Lane (London), soldjer. Bound to John Bare for 10 years in Jamaica.   Age 11.   Sept. 8, 1685. Witness Elizabeth, his mother.   14/393

B

BAGLEY, Thomas. Son of Ralph Bagley, Fleet Street, London. "By the consent of John Dixon his father-in-law and Mary Dixon his mother". Bound to Phillip Gore for 4 years in Jamaica. April 29, 1685.   14/228

BAINHAM, Robert. Son of Thomas Bainham, St. Clement Deanes, Middlesex, taylor, deced. Bound to George Purvis for 8 years in Virginia. Oct. 5, 1685. Witness Mary Armstrong, his mother.   14/425

BAINS, Samuell. Bound to Francis Richardson for 4 years in New Yorke. March 13, 1682.   13

BAISON, Thomas. Son of William Baison of Wick Cambee (Wicken?), Northampton, husbandman, deced. Bound to Thomas Howard for 4 years in Virginia. Age 26. Dec. 2, 1685.   14/466

BAITES, John. Son of Edward Baites of Agmundison (now Amersham), Buckinghamshire. Bound to William Wills for 5 years in Virginia. Nov. 12, 1685.   14/447

BAKER, Mary. Daughter of Gyles Baker of Yarmouth, taylor, deced. Bound to Henry Hawkins for 4 years in Maryland. Aug. 10, 1685.   14/362

BAKER, Thomas. Son of Thomas Baker, St. Georges, Southwark (London), deced. Bound to William Bradley for 5 years in Jamaica. Oct. 27, 1684.
          14/46

BALL, John. Son of John Ball, deced. Bound to Francis Currock for 4 years in Virginia. Oct. 20, 1684.   14/38

BALL, Thomas. Discharged out of Bridewell (prison). Bound to Robert Shanks, marriner, for 4 years in Virginia. Age 23. Nov. 21, 1684.   14/70

BAMFORD, John. Bound to John Hosea for 8 years in Jamaica. Age 13. Oct. 23, 1685. Witness Mary Powell, his mother.   14/438

BANCE, Daniel. A French boy son of John Bance, late of London, buttonmaker. Bound to Marmaduke Larkin for 7 years in Jamaica. Aug. 3, 1685. (See ANBIER).   14/353

BARBADOES, Robert.   "This day his Lordship signed a warrant directed to the sherriffes of London to delivere unto John Harwood and John Saunders or one of them the body of Robert Barbadoes in order to transport him to Barbadoes according to the provisoe in his masters order they having sealed a bond of 100 pounds penalty taken by Mr. Tanner to that purpose".   July 17, 1684.   13

BARBER, George.   Bound to Richard Pattison for 4 years in Jamaica.   Age 27. Dec. 17, 1684.   14/98

BARBER, John.   Kent.   Bound to John Gibbs for 5 years in Carolina.   March 2, 1682.   13

BARNARD, Thomas.   Son of Phillipp Barnard late of Abbaforth (Aberford?), Yorkshire, pipe maker, deced.   Bound to John West for 4 years in Jamaica. Age 20.   Feb. 28, 1684.   16/166

BARNES, John.   Son of Robert Barnes late of London, bricklayer.   Bound to Thomas Stockin for 7 years in Virginia.   Nov. 26, 1685.   14/461

BARNES, Thomas.   Wheelwright.   Bound to John Richardson for 4 years in Pensilvania.   Age 27.   April 6, 1685.   14/213

BARNES, Thomas.   Son of Thomas Barnes, Chichester, butcher, deced. Bound to Richard Moss for 4 years in Maryland.   Aug. 6, 1684.   13

BARON, John.   A Frenchman of London, shoemaker.   Bound to Marmaduke Larkin for 4 years in Jamaica.   Aug. 3, 1685.   (See ANBIER).   14/353

BARTON, John.   Bound to Thomas Saywell for 5 years in Barbadoes.   Age 21. April 8, 1685.   14/214

BARTON, Thomas.   Bound to Samuel Pratt for 4 years in Jamaica.   Nov. 9, 1685.   Witnesses Merrian Day, his sister; Leonard Day, her husband; Francis Thomas, solicitor.   14/445

BASIER, Thomas.   Bound to Christopher Byerly for 7 years in Carolina. Age 16.   Feb. 19, 1685.   14/525

BATTERTON, Thomas.   London.   Labourer.   Bound to Francis and Elizabeth Edwin 7 years in Virginia.   Sept. 30, 1684.   14/22

BAULDRY, Elizabeth.   See BAULDRY, Jean.

BAULDRY, Jean and Elizabeth his wife.   Bound to Marmaduke Larkin for 4 years in Maryland.   August 4, 1685.   (See FLEURIOTT).   14/355

BAXTER, John.   Son of David Baxter, Co. Lancaster, tallow chandler, deced.   Bound to Richard Cox for 4 years in Virginia.   Sept. 5, 1684   13

BAYLEE, Ananias.   Cordwainer.   Bound to Marmaduke Larkin for 4 years in Maryland.   July 23, 1685.   Witness Caleb Dutch, Southwark.   14/338

BAYLY, Elizabeth.   Bound to Marmaduke Larkin for 4 years in Maryland. Aug. 4, 1685.   "Her husband having been before bound".   14/355

BAYNAM, Solomon.   Son of Richard Baynam, weaver, of Spittlefields (London).   Bound to Richard Prissicke for 4 years in Barbadoes.   March 31, 1686.   14/554

BEACHAM, James.   Stratford, Essex.   Smith.   Bound to Rowland Buckley for 4 years in Barbadoes.   April 7, 1685.   14/214

BEALE, Richard.   Barbadoes.   Nov. 15, 1690   15/23

BECKFORD, Peter.   With these servants: Edward Broughton, Anthony Major, Richard Inge, Charles Faller, Mary Farrer, Thomas Allen, John Meales, Dorcas King (?).   Nov. 15, 1690.   Going to Jamaica.   15/22a

BEDDING, Joseph.   Bound to John Moorhead for 4 years in Jamaica.   Age 23.   May 8, 1685.   Witness Ambrose Cox.   See note under Sellby.   14/243

BELCHER, Thomas.   London.   Baker.   Bound to Philip Gower for 4 years in Jamaica.   Age 22.   Unmarried.   April 16, 1685.   14/220

BELGOOD, George.   Son of John Belgood late of Cambridge, deced. Bound to Flachar Dalby for 4 years in Jamaica.   Nov. 4, 1684.   14/49

BELL, John.   Bound to John Robinson for 4 years in Jamaica.   Age 18. May 6, 1686.   Witnesses Thomas Bell, coachman of Maidwell Street, Golding Lane (London?), his father and Mary, his mother.   14

BELL, John.   Bound to Shrimpton or Scrimpton Epephrai? of New England. Nov. 15, 1690   15/23

BENNET, Henry.   Bound to John Robinson for 4 years in Jamaica.   Age 28.
May 6, 1686.   Witness Thomas Hollowell, taylor, Coaleman street(London?).
14

BENNETT, Edward.   Brother of Richard Bennett,   Same details but term of
5 years.   Aug. 18, 1685.   14/371

BENNETT, Richard.   Son of Richard Bennett of Fleet Laine, St. Sepulchers,
London.   Bound apprentice to his father and turned over to Robert Howard
for 4 years in Jamaica.   Aug. 18, 1685.   14/371

BERNARD, John.   Bound to Gilbert Ashley for 4 years in New Providence.
Oct. 22, 1683.   13

BETSON, John.   London.   Pinmaker.   Bound to Robert Forbes for 4 years
in Jamaica.   March 16, 1685.   14/544

BEWITT, John.   Son of Mathew Bewitt of Cheame in Surrey.   To serve
Benjamin Goodwin for 4 years in Jamaica.   Age 17.   Jan. 3, 1684. 14/111

BIGG, Elizabeth.   Daughter of John Bigg of St. Giles, Middlesex, coachman, deced.   Bound to Nathaniel Jones for 4 years in Jamaica.   March 2,
1684.   14/167

BILLING, Mary.   Spinster.   Bound to Samuell Cox for 4 years in Barbadoes.
Age 22.   Dec. 4, 1685   14/486

BIMON, John.   Bound to John Drapentier for 7 years in Virginia.   Age 14.
Sept. 26, 1685.   Witness Elizabeth Bimon of Whitefryers (London), his
mother.   14/419

BIRD, Sarah.   Spinster.   Bound to Aronesto Keckerbecke for 4 years in
Jamaica.   Of full age.   July 21, 1685.   14/334

BLACKLOCK, Robert and MARTIN, John.   Pass to Barbadoes.   Nov. 10,
1690.   15/19

BLAIZE, George.   Bound to Robert Forbes for 4 years in Jamaica.   Age 32.
April 20, 1686.   14/606

BLAND, James.   Pernith (Penrith), Cumberland.   Glazier and plummer.
Bound to William Dockwra for 4 years in "The province of East New Jersey"
Age 22.   March 17, 1684   14/189

8

BLATON, John.   Bound to John Clarke for 5 years in Virginia.   Age 15.
Sept. 21, 1685.   Witness Ellinor Wilson of Newgate (London), his aunt.

14/409

BOICE, Sarah.   Daughter of Rowland Boice, Worcester City, clothier, decd.
Bound to Sebastian Gingee for 4 years in Virginia.   Aug. 4, 1684.   13

BOILL, John.   Bound to Josias Leech for 4 years in Barbadoes.   Age 22.
June 3, 1686.   Witness Richard Lawrence. St. Pauls, Shadwell (London),
wherry man.   14

BOLTON, Edward.   Bound to Phillipp Quinton for 4 years in Barbadoes.
Age 21.   Feb. 9, 1685.   14/517

BOOTH, Charles.   Son of Charles Booth of Sheffan (Shelton or Shifnal?),
Shropshire.   Bound to John Moorhead for 4 years in Jamaica.   Age 20.
May 2, 1685.   Witness Elizabeth Hamond, Smithfield (London) had known
him last two years.   14/232

BOOTH, Elizabeth.   Hackney, Middlesex.   Daughter of Thomas Booth,
late of Clapton, Middlesex, deced.   Bound to Joseph Athy for 4 years in
Mountserrat.   Age 23.   Feb 1, 1685.   Witness William Bradshaw.   (Same
entry as Hester Paine).   14/510

BOULD, William.   Son of Thomas Bould of Ganthrop (Ganthorpe), Yorkshire, clothier.   Bound to John Underlay for 4 years in Nevis.   Witness
Thomas Stapleton his cozen.   Oct. 5, 1685.   14/423

BOWELL, Diana.   Spinster.   Daughter of Robert Bowell, late of Bath in
Wells (probably Bath and Wells, Somerset), deced.   Bound to Thomas
Thackster for 4 years in New England.   Witness Richard Williams of
Golding Lane, weaver in Bridgewater Buildings (probably London).
May 4, 1685.   14/236

BOWSTON, Mary, widow.   Daughter of John Williams of Spittlefields,
(London) deced.   Bound to William Levett for 4 years in Barbadoes.
Age 29.   Dec. 4, 1685.   14/468

BOWTELL, Joseph.   Bound to Richard Jackson for 4 years in Barbadoes.
Oct. 15, 1684.   14/31

BOYLSTON, Anne.   London.   Spinster.   Bound to Samuell Roberts for

9

4 years in Maryland.   Aug. 2, 1684.   13

BRADLEY, George.   Bound to James Bowman for 3 years in Barbadoes.
Aug. 21, 1684.   13

BRADLEY, John.   Son of Simon Bradley of Worcester (County), yeoman.
Bound to Roger Giles for 4 years in Virginia.   Oct. 15, 1684.   14/31

BRADSHAW, James.   Bound to John Williams for 4 years in Barbadoes.
Age 24.   March 13, 1684.   14/183

BRATHWAITE, Thomas.   Son of Simon Brathwaite of Ripping (Ripon?),
Yorkshire, butcher, deced.   Bound to John Gibbs for 5 years in Carolina.
Feb. 20, 1682.   13

BRAY, Elizabeth.   Spinster.   Bound to Jeremiah Hawthorne for 5 years in
Barbadoes.   Age 20.   June 11, 1686.   14

BRAY, Elizabeth.   Daughter of William Bray of London, bricklayer "by
the consent of Elizabeth her mother".   Bound to Joseph Bartholomew for
4 years in Jamaica.   Age 17.   April 13, 1685   14/219

BRAY, Rachaell.   Daughter of Charles Bray of Farrington, Berkshire, free-
mason, deced.   Bound to William Lawes for 4 years in Jamaica.   Age 18.
April 22, 1685.   14/221

BRAY, Richard.   Bound to Charles Richards for 4 years in Jamaica.   Age 22.
April 19, 1686.   14/605

BRAYWOOD, Sarah.   Bound to Henry Sutton for 4 years in Carolina.
March 7, 1682.   13

BREADCOTT, Mary.   Daughter of Richard Breadcott of Dorchester, Oxfordshire, marriner, deced.   Bound to John Heslewood for 6 years in Virginia.
July 16, 1684.   13

BRENT, Elizabeth.   Bound to Philip Clarke for 4 years in Maryland.
July 25, 1684.   13

BRERY, John.   Late of Ot(t)ley, Yorkshire.   "Being lately disbanded out of
millitary service".   Bound to Fitzwilliam Lawrence for 4 years in Virginia.
July 23, 1685.   14/337

10

BRETT, Elizabeth.   Bound to John Drapentier for 8 years in Virginia.
Age 12.   Sept. 26, 1685.   Witness Elizabeth Brett her mother, Whitefryers (London).   14/419

BRIDGMAN, Richard.   Hertford.   Bound to James Harding for 7 years in
Jamaica.   Aug. 6, 1685.   14/357

BRINKWELL, Isaiah.   Son of John Brinkwell of Petty Coate Lane, Whitechapple (London).   Bound to James Foster for 7 years in Mount Serratt.
April 2, 1685.   (He and Frances EVES bound themselves on the affirmation
of William Morgin of Bishopsgate Streete, London, blacksmith and Anne
Baylchin, widow, "that their relaciouns were all dead and that they were
not apprentices nor married but went of their own free and voluntary accord".
See also Thomas MORGIN)   14/209

BRISCO, Nathaniel.   Shoemaker.   Bound to Richard Heath for 4 years in
Maryland.   Age 21.   Aug. 2, 1684.   13

BROADWATER, Thomas.   Son of Robert Broadwater of St. Mary, Newing-
ham (ton?), Surry.   Bound to Thomas Hunt for 4 years in Jamaica.   March 2,
1684.   16/167

BROOKE, Joseph.   Glass bottle maker.   Bound to Joseph Martin for 4 years
in Pensilvania.   Sept. 4, 1684.   (Same details exactly as James HARRIS)
                                                               13

BROOKES, Anne.   Daughter of Richard Brookes, Stamford, Lincolnshire,
baker, deced.   Bound to John Payne for 4 years in Maryland.   Age 20.
Aug. 11, 1685.   Witness Katherine Fraizby, London, known her 4 years.
                                                               14/364

BROOKES, William.   Son of William Brookes of Great Whitley, (Witley),
Worcestershire, husbandman.   Bound to Christopher Ronsby for 4 years in
Maryland.   July 22, 1684.   13

BROUGH, James.   Bound to Alexander Rowland for 5 years in Jamaica.
Age 13.   March 15, 1685.   Witness Sarah, his mother.   14/544

BROUGHTON, Edward.   See BECKFORD, Peter.

BROWNE, Dukesell.   Son of John Browne of Herreford, carrier, deced.
Bound to John Haslewood for 10 yrs. in Virginia.   July 4, 1684.   (See
HARDING, Henry).   13

BROWNE, Edward. Bound to Thomas Hunt for 4 years in Jamaica. Age 21 March 12, 1684. 14/181

BROWNE, Edward. Bound to Robert Shanks for 4 years in Jamaica. Age 21. Nov. 20, 1684. 14/69

BROWN(E), Elizabeth. Daughter of Thomas Browne of London, cornchandler, deced. Bound to Richard Feversom for 4 years in Maryland. Aug. 31, 1685. Witness Dorothy her mother. 14/386

BROWNE, Elizabeth. Daughter of William Browne, London, bricklayer, deced. Bound to Ffossett Gardner for 5 years in Virginia. Nov. 9, 1685. Witness Thomas Buttler, gent. of Clerkenwell Green, brother-in-law of Gardner. "Elizabeth was comitted thither (Clerkenwell prison) for pilfering some small things and was since discharged and was desirous to go beyond seas". 14/445

BROWNE, Elizabeth. Bound to Edward Bennett (probably should read Richard Bennett - compare with Richard and Edward Bennett) and handed over to Robert Howard for 4 years in Jamaica. Aug. 18, 1685. Consent of Elizabeth Townsend her sister and John Townsend, brother-in-law. 14/371

BROWNE, Grace. Daughter of Richard Browne of St. Andrews, Holborne, London. Bound to Robert Burman for 5 years in Maryland. July 25, 1685. Witnesses her father and Katherine her mother. 14/340

BROWNE, James of London. Labourer. Bound to Robert Shanks for 4 years in Jamaica. Age 21. Nov. 27, 1684. 14/75

BROWNE, Joane. Bound to John Robinson for 4 years in Jamaica. Age 19. May 1, 1686. Witness Mary Trevailer. (See Rebeccah Robinson). 14/621

BROWNE, Ralph. of London. Labourer. Bound to Christopher Byerley for 4 years in Carolina. Feb. 19, 1685. Witness Robert Chesman his half brother. 14/525

BROWNE, Sara. Bound to James Foster for 4 years in Mount Serratt. Age 21. April 9, 1685. 14/216

BUCK, Gabriel. Bound to Robert Shanks for 4 years in Jamaica. Age 21. Nov. 21, 1684. 14/70

BULL, Katherine of Shoreditch, Middlesex. Spinster. Bound to Christopher Jefferson for 5 years in St. Christophers. Age 24. Dec. 19, 1683. 13

BULLOCK, Mary. Daughter of John Bullock of Benson in Oxfordshire. Bound to Phillipp Gore (probably Gower) for 4 years in Jamaica. Age 22. April 1, 1685. 14/206

BURCH, Solomon. Son of John Burch of Guildford, Surry, clarke, deced. Bound to John Payne for 13 years in Maryland. Aug. 11, 1685. Witness Elizabeth Burch his mother. 14/364

BURCH, Timothy. Bound to James Finch for 7 years in Pennsilvania. April 1, 1686. Witness William Burch his brother. 14/556

BURGIS, John. Bound to Jonathan Matthews for 4 years in Virginia. Aug. 23. 1684. 13

BURNELL, Margaret. Spinster. Bound to William Bird for 4 years in Nevis. Age 19. Oct. 2, 1685, 14/421

BURNETT, John. Bound to Barnaby Cater for 4 years in Barbadoes. April 28, 1685. 14/227

BURNLEY, Peter. Bound to George Norris for 4 years in Maryland. Age 21. Aug. 29, 1685. Witness Enoch Bennister of Canterbury. 14/385

BURROUGHS, John, of Shoreditch, Middlesex. Labourer. Bound to John Richards for 4 years in Barbadoes. Oct. 27, 1684. 14/45

BUSBY, John and DAVIS, William. Pass to Pensilvania. Nov. 10, 1690. 15/19

BUTCHER, John. "A pass for John Butcher to go to New England, the ship called the Mary of Boston of which John Gardner is master upon the testimony of Nichas Strange, Paternoster Row, taylor". July 5, 1685. 14/317

BUTCHER, Thomas. Servant of Veysey, Richard, q. v.

BUTLER, Rebecca of St. Giles in the Fields, Middlesex. Spinster. Bound to Thomas Niccolls for 4 years in Jamaica. Age 24. June 8, 1685. "By consent of Margery Butler her mother". 14/275

13

BUTTERFIELD, Elizabeth.   Daughter of John Butterfield late of Gravesend (Kent), waterman, deced.   Bound to Christopher Eyre for 4 years in Jamaica. May 6, 1685.   Witness Margaret Bradley of Shadwell Dock.   14/238

BUTTLER, Edward.   Son of John Buttler of Ailscowan (?) in Essex.   Bound to Richard Bent for 4 years in   Virginia.   Nov. 11, 1684   14/56

BUTTON, Mary of London.   Spinster.   Bound to Thomas Niccolls for 4 years in Jamaica.   Age 20.   Sept. 28, 1685.   14/420

BUXTON, William.   Son of William Buxton of Southwark, gardner, deced. Bound to John Haslewood for 9 years in Virginia.   July 28, 1684.   13

C

CALIGNON, Edward; PATRONE, Jean Louys; SOUX, Augustine; GUESHARD, Samuel. Bound apprentice to James Boullay planter of Maryland. Came before his Lordship according to his Majesty's late order to prevent spiriting and declared themselves willing to serve their said master according to their indentures. (No terms stated). Jan. 19, 1682.   13

CANCKLEY, Thomas. Son of Abraham Canckley of Newbolt (Newbold) in Leicester, labourer. Bound to David Lockwood for 5 years in Jamaica. Nov. 13, 1684.   14/58

CAPPUR, Philippus. Son of Harrington Cappur of London, Gent. Bound to Philip Gower for 7 years in Jamaica "by consent of his father". June 1, 1685.
                    14/270

CARMELL, Thomas. Bound to John Williams for 4 years in Barbadoes. Age 28. March 13, 1684.   14/183

CARRICKE, Charles. Bound to Francis Foxcroft for 4 years in Boston, New England. April 24, 1686. Witness John Smith.   14/609

CARTER, Henry. Bound to Robert Burman for 6 years in Maryland. July 14, 1684.   13

CARTER, Thomas. Son of William Carter, citizen and cook of London, deced. Bound to Emmanuel Hutson for 7 years in Barbados. May 16, 1683.
                    13

CARVER, Robert. Son of Richard Carver of Westminster, deced. Bound to John Burton for 9 years in Virginia. July 29, 1685. Witnesses Edward Crosse and John Clarke.   14/347

CARTWRIGHT, Sybilla, spinster. Bound to Francis White in Virginia (No term stated). Oct. 19, 1683.   13

CASH, John. Son of Thomas Cash of Jamaica, planter. Bound to Richard Heath for 7 years in Maryland. July 11, 1684.   13

CAWDREY, Ethell, spinster. Bound to Thomas Gadsden for 4 years in Virginia. Age 20. Feb. 10, 1685. 14/519

CHABET, Peter and FANEUIL, Andrew. Two French Protestants going to Boston, New England. Nov. 14, 1690. 15/22a

CHALLENOR, Thomas. Son of Arthur Challenor of Lysborne, Yorkshire, gent. Bound to Phillipp Gower for 4 years in Jamaica. March 2, 1684. 14/167

CHAMBERLAINE, William. Son of William Chamberlaine late of Stroud-water, Gloucestershire, deced. Bound to Emmanuel Windsor for 7 years in New Yorke. Age 14. March 19, 1684. 14/192

CHAMBERLEN, Francis. Son of Edward Chamberlen late of Dublin, Ireland, shoemaker. Bound to David Lockwood for 4 years in Jamaica. Nov. 4, 1684. 14/49

CHAPMAN, Henry. Son of Henry Chapman of Harford, weaver. (Could be Harford, Devon or Hertford, Herts. or Hereford). Bound to Edward Brook for 4 years in Jamaica. Oct. 18, 1684. 14/35

CHARNLY, William. Going to Barbadoes and Antego. Nov. 10, 1690
15/19a

CHERREY, Francis. Son of Francis Cherrey of Chollingtrey (Collingtree), Northamptonshire, deced. Bound to William Goring for 5 years in Barbadoes. Age 14. April 14, 1685. "Neither father nor mother living". 14/219

CHETWIN, Thomas. London. Labourer. Bound to John West for 4 years in Jamaica. Age 24. March 17, 1684. "Has neither wife nor child".
14/189

CHIDLEY, Katherine, spinster. Bound to Mathew Trim for 4 years in Virginia. Age 24. Dec. 14, 1685. Witnesses Stephen Michell her brother, Whitechapple (London), taylor. 14/479

CHILDE, Matthias, son of Matthias Childe of London Wall, silkman, deced. Bound to Thomas Baylee for 4 years in Carolina near Virginia. Dec. 7, 1685. Witness Margrett Childe, his mother. 14/473

CHITTY, Richard. "With his wife, son and maidservant". Going to Jamaica. Nov. 11, 1690. 15/20

CITTERSON, Nicholas.   Bound to Abraham Wilde for 4 years in Maryland.
Aug. 21, 1684.   13

CLARK, John.   Son of John Clark of Barking, Essex, woolcomber, deced.
Bound to George Elkin for 7 years in Jamaica.   Sept. 3, 1685.   Witnesses
Thomas Franck, Edward English, William Walford, Overseers of the Poor of
Barking.   14/389

CLARKE, John.   Son of John Clarke of the Minnoryes, London.   Bound to
William Martin for 4 years in Jamaica.   Dec. 31, 1684.   14/109

CLARKE, John.   Son of John Clarke of Suffolk, weaver.   Bound to Edward
Brook for 4 years in Jamaica.   Oct. 18, 1684.   (Same entry as Henry
CHAPMAN).   14/35

CLARKE, Mary, spinster.   Bound to John Rudds for 4 years in Virginia.
Age 18.   Sept. 22, 1685.   Witness Margaret Gollan, her mother.   14/410

CLARKE, Mary, spinster.   Daughter of John Clarke of London, shoemaker.
Bound to Richard Jackson for 4 years in Barbadoes.   Oct. 15, 1684.   14/31

CLARKE, Robert.   Bound to Richard Abbott for 3 years in Nevis.   Age 27.
Oct. 25, 1684.   14/43

CLARKSON, Richard.   Bound to John Moorhead for 4 years in Jamaica.
Age 26.   May 5, 1685.   Witness Joseph Randall, Monmouth Street in St.
Giles (London), joyner.   14/237

CLARLY, George.   Bound to John Seaman for 4 years in Maryland.   Age 52.
July 27, 1685.   (See also John JONES and Joshua HARTLEY).   14/344.

CLAY, Robert.   Son of John Clay, Norwich.   Bound to Thomas Tenche for
4 years in Maryland.   Aug. 13, 1684.   13

CLAYSON, Charles.   Bound to John Munford for 4 years in Virginia.   Age 21.
Dec. 14, 1685.   Witnesses Francis Claysan and Katherine, his mother of
Dyers Yard, Old Bedlam.   14/478

CLAYTON, John.   Son of Richard Clayton of Bloomsbury, Middlesex, baker.
"With the consent of Jane Clayton, his mother".   Bound to Thomas Cason
for 9 years in Virginia.   Oct. 6, 1684.   14/26

CLERKE, Ellenor of London, spinster. Bound to Thomas Clark for 4 years in Barbadoes. Age 21. Dec. 16, 1684. 14/95

CLIFFORD, Suzanna, spinster. Bound to Alice Bare for 4 years in Nevis. Age 17. Nov. 19, 1685. Witness Suzanna Clifford, her mother, Holborne (London). 14/453

CLITHEROE, Robert of Litleplun, Co. of Lancaster (Little Poulton or Litherland or Liverpool?). Bound to John Nugent for 4 years in Jamaica. Age 24. Jan. 8, 1684. 14/115

COATES, Mary. Bound to Bartholemew Sprint for 4 years in New York. Age 18. June 11, 1686. 14

COBBY, Robert. Son of Robert Cobby of Buckingham Town, maltster, deced. Bound to Thomas Tench for 7 years in Maryland. Aug. 12, 1684. 13

COCKIN, Jane. Bound to Thomas Colebeech for 4 years in Virginia. March 1, 1685. Witness Mary Davies, (mother of Mary Davies, q.v. which is on the same entry). 14/533

COE, Susanna. Daughter of Andrew Coe of London, printer, deced. Bound to Philipp Clarke for 5 years in Maryland. Aug. 6, 1684. 13

COGGILL, Mary of London, spinster. Bound to Matthew Trim for 5 years in Virginia. Nov. 19, 1684. 14/68

COLDWELL, John, son of William Coldwell, late of Black Barnsley in Yorkshire (probably Barnsley). Bound to John Peirson for 4 years in Jamaica. Age 28, unmarried. Nov. 5, 1684. 14/87

COLE, Jonathan, being a poor boy left in the parish of Coleshurst, London, in the presence of Mr. Thomas Hanwell one of the churchwardens of the said parish, bound himself to Thomas Gadsden of Limehouse in the parish of Stepney, County of Middlesex, marriner, to serve him in Barbadoes 7 years". July 20, 1685. 14/331

COLE, Richard. Bound to Thomas Ackerman for 4 years in Virginia. Age 21. Jan. 11, 1685. 14/495

COLLINS, James. Son of John Collins of Woolvercott, Oxfordshire, labourer,

deced.   "Being an idle boy taken up in the streets voluntarily became
bound. . . . " to John Lightfoot for 12 years in Virginia. July 7, 1684.   13

COLLINS, John.   Son of Robert Collins late of Farrington in Dorsett, deced.
Bound to Phillipp Gower for 4 years in Jamaica.   Age 20.   May 22, 1685.
                                                                                                            14/260

COLLINS, Samuel.   Bound to John Richards for 4 years in Barbadoes.
Age 21.   Nov. 19, 1684.   14/68

COLLINS, William, of Kent.   Carpenter.   Bound to James Williams for 4
years in Jamaica.   April 2, 1685.   14/209

COMBES, John.   Bound to Daniell Duthaes for 7 years in Pensilvania.
March 26, 1684.   13

CONNOR, Richard.   Bound to John Paine for 4 years in Maryland.   Age 21.
Sept. 23, 1685.   14/414

COOK, Henry.   Son of John Cook of St. Giles in the Fields (Middlesex),
butcher, deced.   Bound to Solomon Niccolls for 4 years in Maryland.
Age 19.   Sept. 4, 1685.   Witness Elizabeth Cook, his sister.   14/390

COOKE, Mary.   Daughter of Thomas Cooke, blacksmith, near St. Thomases
Hospital, Southwarke (Surrey).   Bound to Godfrey Cumin for 4 years in
Jamaica.   May 28, 1686.   Witnesses her father and Lucee, her mother.   14

COOKE, Thomas.   Son of Samuel Cooke, Stepney, Middlesex, weaver.
Bound to Arnesto Kackerbart for 5 years in Virginia.   July 27, 1685.   14/343

COOPER, Margaretta Maria, spinster.   Bound to John and Elizabeth Haynes
for 4 years in Maryland.   July 27, 1685.   Witness Mrs. White.   14/345

CORE, Elizabeth of London, spinster.   Bound to Richard Heath for 4 years
in Maryland.   Age 17.   July 6, 1685.   14/317

CORNISH, Elizabeth, spinster.   Bound to John Wiseman for 4 years in
Virginia.   Age 25.   Oct. 24, 1684.   14/42

CORNISH, Michael.   Son of Michael Cornish, late of Drury Lane (London),
joiner, deced.   Bound to John Williams for 4 years in Jamaica.   Witnesses
Peter Cheltenham of Noble street, joyner, his master and Thomas Watson

Guardian one of his father's executors. May 4, 1685. 14/236

COTMORE, James. Son of James Cotmore of St. Giles without Cripplegate (London), victualler. Bound to John Bawdon for 3 years in Nevis. "To serve in the quality of a cooper". Dec. 28, 1683. 13

COTSWELL, Robert. Son of Thomas Cotswell deced. Bound to John Dikes for 6 years in Barbadoes. April 8, 1685. 14/214

COTTAM, Richard. London. Vintner. Bound to Gregory Dorset for 4 years in Barbadoes. Nov. 18, 1685. 14/453

CRADOCK, Martha, widow. Midwife. Bound to John Gibbs for 4 years in Carolina. March 2, 1682. 13

CRAINE, Robert. "having been formerly beyond seas". Bound to Arthur Smith for 3 years in Antego. Age 30. Nov. 12, 1685. 14/447

CRANE, Mary. Daughter of John Crane of St. Martins le Grand, London, shoemaker, deced. Bound to John Heslewood for 6 years in Virginia. July 16, 1684. 13

CRESSILL, John. Son of Phillipp Cressill, weaver, Colchester, Essex, deced. Bound to John Burgis for 6 years in Virginia. Aug. 15, 1684. 13

CRISPE, Pheasant and his servant. Going to Jamaica. June 22, 1691. 15/39a

CROPPIN, William of Rixham (Brixham?), Devon. "Being a lusty young man about 26 years old and verrie desirous to go over sea". Bound to Arthur Smith for 3 years in Antego. Nov. 12, 1685. 14/447

CROSS, Joshua. Son of Joshua Cross late Der (Debter?) of (place undecipherable), deced. Bound to Samuel Hanson for 4 years in Barbadoes. Oct. 1, 1684. 14/23

CROSSE, John. Son of Leonard Crosse of Newgate Street, London. Bound to Margaret Chelderey of Newgate St. and assigned to Michael Tauny of Maryland for 9 years in Maryland. Sept. 14, 1685. Witness Jane Crosse, his mother. 14/400

CRUYKSHANCKS, John. Bound to Nicholas Dove for 3 years in Jamaica.

Nov. 26, 1685. 14/460

CUCKENFEILD, Thomas.   Son of William Cuckenfeild of Brinle (Brindle?) in Lancashire.   Bound to David Lockwood for 4 years in Jamaica.   Nov. 14, 1684. 14/59

CUNYNGHAM, Robert.   Barbadoes.   Servant to Wm. Harris.   Nov. 13, 1690. 15/21a

CURD, Mary.   Daughter of William Curd late of London.   Bound to Robert Shanks for 4 years in Jamaica.   Sept. 29, 1684. 14/22

CURTIS, Isabella, spinster.   Bound to Aronesto Keckerbecke for 4 years in Virginia.   Of full age.   July 21, 1685. 14/335

D

DAINE, John. Son of John Daine, late of Sherborne (No county), gardener, deced. Bound to David Lockwood for 4 years in Jamaica. Nov. 8, 1684.
14/52

DAINTYE, Katherine. Daughter of William Daintye. Bound to Nathaniel Anderton and assigned to John Abbington for 5 years in Maryland. Aug. 20, 1685. Witness Ellenor Daintye, her mother.
14/374

DANSTER, Sarah. Daughter of William Danster of Southam, Warwickshire, joiner. Bound to Nicholas Crainsborough for 4 years in Virginia. Nov. 8, 1684.
14/52

DARSON, Edmond. Son of James Darson of Shrewsbury, Shropshire, farmer. Bound to Christopher Jefferson for 4 years in St. Christophers. Feb. 23, 1685.
14/529

DAUGHTON or DAUGTON, Thomas. Son of Thomas Daughton of Nightingale Lane, East Smithfield (London), tobacco pipe maker. Bound to Daniell Claphamson for 8 years in Maryland. Aug. 13, 1685.
14/366

DAVENPORT, Adington. Going to New England. Nov. 15, 1690.
15/23

DAVENPORT, Edward. Waltham Cross, Hertford. Labourer. Bound to Samuel Gilham for 4 years in Virginia. Aug. 10, 1683.
13

DAVESON, Grace. Daughter of Henry Daveson of Plimouth, marriner, deced. Bound to Richard Flye for 5 years in Maryland. Aug. 11, 1684.
13

DAVIES, Elizabeth. Daughter of William Davies of Oakley (Ockley), Surrey. husbandman, deced. Bound to Thomas Davies for 4 years in Barbadoes. (Same entry as Elizabeth Jackman). June 17, 1686
14

DAVIES, Elizabeth of Bristol, spinster. Bound to Robert Barrington for 4 years in West Indies. Age 22. Jan 7, 1684.
14/114

DAVIES, James. Son of Hugh Davies, husbandman of Devon. Bound to

Phillipp Hodge for 4 years in Jamaica.   Age 21.   March 30, 1686.   14/553

DAVIES, Joseph.   Son of Thomas Davies of Long Alley, London.   Bound to Humphrey Buncarr for 4 years in Virginia.   Nov. 11, 1684.   14/56

DAVIES, Mary.   Daughter of Mary Davies of Clare Markett in Bear Yard (London?)   Bound to Thomas Colebeech for 4 years in Virginia.   March 1, 1885.   Witness Mary Davies her mother.   (See Jane Cockin)   14/533

DAVIES, Thomas.   Son of Richard Davies of Bristow, (Bristol?), merchant, deced.   "Came before his lordship and did acknowledge himselfe to be the apprentice of Richard Stephens since Nov. 7, 1684.   Bound for 3 years. Aug. 10, 1685.   No destination given.   14/361

DAVIES, William.   Son of Richard Davies of St. Martins in the Fields, marriner, deced.   Bound to John Underlay for 4 years in Virginia.   Oct. 5, 1685.   Witness Jane Wybourne, his aunt.   14/424

DAVIS, Mary.   Daughter of Francis Davis.   Bound to William Flood for 4 years in Jamaica.   Oct. 24, 1684.   14/42

DAVIS, William.   See John BUSBY.

DAVIS, William.   See Elizabeth HUMES.

DAVIS, William.   Son of William Davis of Barnett in Middlesex, starch-maker, deced.   Bound to Thomas Tench for 7 years in Maryland.   July 25, 1684.   13

DAVISON, Phillis of London, spinster.   Bound to John Moorhead for 4 years in Jamaica.   May 4, 1685.   Witness Mary Cox of Pennington Street, Ratcliffe (London).   14/236

DAVYES, Hugh.   Son of Richard Davyes of Portsmouth, gunner, deced. Bound to David Lockwood for 4 years in Jamaica.   Oct. 7, 1684.   14/51

DAY, Agnes of London, spinster.   Bound to Alice Bare for 4 years in Nevis. Age 16.   Nov. 24, 1685.   Witness Elizabeth Franklyn.   14/459

DAY, Elizabeth.   "Wife of Stephen Day, sawyer, bound by consent of her husband..."   Bound to Andrew Herring for 4 years in Virginia.   Dec. 18, 1684.   14/99

DAY, Robert. Late of Norwich, now of London, weaver. Bound to John Burroughs of Northampton County in Arromack in Virginia, merchant for 4 years in Virginia. Aug. 9, 1683. 13

DEBEARE, James, of Barwicke (Berwick) upon Tweed, taylor. "Being a stout young man, etc." (See William CROPPIN). Bound to Edward Williams for 4 years in Jamaica. Nov. 12, 1685. 14/449

DECASSERIS, Abraham, his wife, son and daughter. Going to Barbadoes. Nov. 10, 1690. (Same entry as Isaac DECASSERIS and David MACHERE). 15/19a

DECASSERIS, Isaac. Going to Jamaica. Nov. 10, 1690. (Same entry as Abraham DECASSERIS) 15/19a

DELAMOTT, Margrett of Isle of Wight, Hampshire, now of London, spinster. Bound to John Robinson for 4 years in Jamaica. Age 26. May 1, 1686. Witness Phillipp Atkins of Spittlefeilds (London), taylor. (Same entry as Anne HAYNE). 14/621

DENNIS, James. Son of James Dennis of Whitechapple, London, deced. Bound to John Burman for 8 years in Maryland. July 21, 1685. Witness Elizabeth Davis, his mother. 14/332

DENNIS, John. Son of Thomas Dennis, late of Higham in Kent. Bound to Robert Cox for 9 years in Virginia. Oct. 9, 1684. 14/29

DENTON, Charles. Bound to John Barry for 5 years in Barbadoes. Sept. 24, 1684. 14/18

DESHAWNS, Abraham, son of James Deshawns of Germany. Bound to Augustin Boullay for 7 years in Maryland. Sept. 15, 1685. Witness William Allor of Bishopsgate Street (London). 14/401

DEVONPORT, James. Son of Edward Devonport of Reedcroft Street, London, printer. Bound to William Tyleby for 10 years in Jamaica. Age 10. Jan. 25, 1685. 14/504

DEWHURST, Richard, of London, labourer. Bound to Henry Low for 4 years in Maryland. Age 30. Nov. 29, 1684. 14/78

DICKEN, Thomas of Cainoack (Cannock?), Staffordshire, but now of London.

Bound to Clement Tidway for 3 years in Antigua. Term to be served from March 25 next (i.e. beginning of 1686 old style). Jan. 22, 1685.   14/501

DICKINS, Jonathan of Stepney, Middlesex, bricklayer. Bound to John Netherway for 4 years in Nevis. Jan 23, 1684. No wife or children.

14/133

DIXON, William. Bound to Robert Roadds for 4 years in Jamaica. Age 22. May 5, 1685. Witness John Wadley of Deptford (London), waterman   14/237

DODD, Simon. Son of Thomas Dodd of Newcastle in Staffordshire, deced, shoemaker. Bound to John West for 4 years in Jamaica. Age 31. Feb. 28, 1684.   14/166

DOVE, Arthur. Son of Humfrey Dove of London, gentleman. Bound to Thomas Wyche for 4 years in Carolina. May 16, 1683.   13

DOWNES, John. Son of Samuell Downes of Lincolne City, deced. Bound to Thomas Tench for 4 years in Maryland. Aug. 12, 1684.   13

DOWNES, William. Son of James Downes in Basinghall Street, London. Bound to Michaell Petry and Thomas Laine for 4 years in Virginia or elsewhere. July 22, 1684.   13

DOWZIN, John. Labourer. Bound to James Williams for 4 years in Barbadoes. Age 21. May 11, 1686.   14

DOYLEY, Lavinia. Daughter of Edward Doyley, late of Bloomsbury, Holborne (London), deced. Bound to Philip Gore for 4 years in Jamaica. April 29, 1685.   14/228

DRAPER, John of London, clothmaker. Bound to Andrew Ker for 4 years in Barbadoes. Feb. 19, 1685. Witness Samuel Draper of Broad Street, his father.   14/525

DRUNCKCOURT, James. Son of Antho. Drunckcourt of Quaker Street, Spittlefeilds, (London), Reedmaker. Bound to Samuel Roberts for 7 years in Maryland. Witnesses Anthony, his father and Susanna, his mother. Sept. 14, 1685.   14/400

DUNCKLEY, Elizabeth. Bound to George Wilson for 4 years in Maryland. Age 22. Aug. 28, 1685.   14/383

DUNMOORE or DUNMORE, Margrett.   Daughter of Richard Dunmore,
Innholder, London.   Bound to William Bennett for 5 years in Virginia.
Dec. 9, 1685.   Thomas Bennett (a physician) affirmed she had the consent
of her father who was in prison.   14/474

DYKE, John, of Catstock (?), Dorsett, labourer.   Bound to Robert Shanks
for 4 years in Jamaica.   Sept. 29, 1684.   14/22

E

EADES, Elizabeth.   Sister of Thomas Eades, q. v.   Bound to Myles Staples for 4 years in Maryland.   Age 23.   Aug. 14, 1685.   14/369

EADES, Henry.   Son of Henry Eades of Godmanchester, Huntingdonshire. taylor, deced.   Bound to John Lightfoot for 7 years in Virginia.   July 14, 1684.   13

EADES, Peter.   Son of Peter Eades of Butcher Row, White Chapple (London), cooper, deced.   Bound to David Lockwood for 4 years in Jamaica.   Nov. 7, 1684.   (Follows Hugh DAVYES).   14/51

EADES, Thomas and (Elizabeth Eades) son (and daughter) of John Eades of Wellsborne Munford, Warwickshire, gentleman, deced.   Bound to Myles Staples for 4 years in Maryland.   Age 20.   Aug. 14, 1685.   14/369

EAKINS, Jonathan.   Son of Richard Eakins, late of London, deced.   Bound to Nicholas Smith for 6 years in Maryland.   Age 14.   Aug. 4, 1685.   14/354

EAST, Francis.   Bound to Phillip Redwood for 4 years in Tobago.   Aug. 25, 1683.   13

EASTOP, Joseph.   Son of John Eastop, late of London, glover, deced. Bound to Mathew Daveson for 5 years in Maryland.   Aug. 26, 1685. Witness Richard Eaton.   14/381

EDDINGTON, Robert.   Son of Thomas Eddington of Lorgersunt, Wiltshire. (Ludgershall?), broadcloth weaver, deced.   Bound to James Fidler for 4 years in Virginia.   Age 33.   Dec. 5, 1685.   14/469

EDLINGTON, John.   Son of Henry Edlington, late of London, deced. Bound to Seager Walter for 7 years in Jamaica.   Nov. 17, 1684.   14/64

EDMOND, Thomas.   Going to Barbadoes.   Nov. 15, 1690   15/23

EDWARDS, Jane.   See Anne SIMONDS.

EDWARDS, Jane.   Daughter of John Edwards of Tame (Thame), Oxfordshire.

Shoe maker, deced. Bound to Ernesto Keckerbart for 4 years in Virginia.
Age 23. Aug. 11, 1685. 14/364

EDWARDS, Mary, of London, spinster. Bound to Joseph Bartholemew for
4 years in Jamaica. Age 23. April 14, 1685. 14/219

ELLETT, Peter. Son of Thomas Ellett of London, deced. Bound to Mary
Rosewell for 3 years in Jamaica. Sept. 5, 1685. 14/391

ELLGOOD, Richard of Market Peareham (Pulham Market ?), Norfolk, labourer. Bound to John Pye for 4 years in Jamaica. Jan. 8, 1684. 14/116

ELLIOT, Stephen. Going to Jamaica. Nov. 10, 1690. 15/19a

ELLIOT, William. Pass to Merryland and New Jersey. ·March 6, 1690.
15/31

ELLISON, George. Son of William Ellison of St. Olaves, Southwark (Surrey).
Bound to William Mingham for 5 years in Jamaica. June 2, 1684. 13

ELLSEY, Thomas, millwright. Son of Thomas Ellsey, husbandman of
Leicestershire. Bound to John Pikes for 4 years in Jamaica. March 7,
1684. 14/171

ELLWOOD, Cipper. Bound to Thomas Sawell for 5 years in Jamaica.
May 28, 1685. 14/265

ENG, Ann. Daughter of William Eng, clarke, deced. Bound to Anthony
Ensdale for 5 years in Jamaica. Oct. 30, 1684. 14/47

ENGLAND, Francis. (No details) July 2, 1683 13

ERVIN, Andrew. Son of Andrew Ervin of Shetland in the Kingdom of
Scotland. Bound to Thomas Ross for 6 years in Barbadoes. Age 16.
Aug 9, 1684. 13

EVANS, John. Son of John Evans late of Aldgate (London), porter, deced.
Bound to George Purvis for 7 years in Virginia. Nov. 3, 1685. Witness
Hellen Evans his mother. 14/441

EVANS, Samuel. Son of Ellis Evans, late of Southwarke (Surrey), deced.
"By consent of his father-in-law Paul Milbourne, living at the further end of

Kent Streete in Southwarke, basketmaker, who declared that the apprentice has neither father nor mother living and was a single man". Bound to John Williams for 4 years in Virginia. Age 21 and upwards. March 16, 1684. 14/189

EVANS, Thomas. Son of Thomas Evans of London, porter, deced. Bound to Thomas Baily for 5 years in North Carolina. Age 18. Dec. 4, 1685. Witness Elizabeth Evans, his mother. 14/468

EVERARD, John. Bound to Christopher Squire for 4 years in Jamaica. Age 23. Nov. 20, 1684. 14/69

EVERLINGS, Gerrard, "late of the Hague in the beyond the seas", shoemaker. Bound to Thomas Hunt for 4 years in Jamaica. Age 20. March 17, 1684. 14/189

EVES, Frances. Daughter of John Eves of Eppin (Epping), Essex. Bound to James Foster for 4 years in Mount Serratt. April 2, 1685. (Under same entry as Brinkwell , q.v.) 14/209

EVES, John. Bound to Francis Edwin for 6 years in Virginia. Sept. 16, 1684. 14/9

F

FAIRLAND, John.   Son of John Fairland of Selby, Yorkshire, yeoman, deced.   Bound to John Brook for 4 years in Virginia.   Age 28.   Oct. 5, 1685.   14/424

FALLER, Charles.   See Peter BECKFORD.

FANEUIL, Andrew.   See Peter CHABET.

FANN or FAN,   Elizabeth, of St. Butt (Botolph?) Without, Bishopsgate, London, spinster.   Bound to Phillipp Clarke for 4 years in Maryland. July 31, 1684.   13

FARRER, Mary.   See Peter BECKFORD.

FARWELL, Elizabeth, spinster.   Bound to James and Margaret Skinner for 4 years in Jamaica.   Sept. 29, 1685.   14/420

FAWNE, George.   Son of George Fawne, Isle of Garnsey (Guernsey), Hamp-shire, woolcomber.   "Consent of his father and mother, they being very poore and not able to maintaine him".   Bound to John Bare for 12 years in Jamaica.   Age 10.   Sept. 8, 1685.   14/393

FEILD, Samuel.   Bound to Charles Richards for 7 years in Jamaica.   March 31, 1686.   Witness Dorothy Feild, his mother.   14/554

FEILD, Thomas.   Going to New England.   Nov. 12, 1690.   15/21a

FEMELL, Richard.   Son of Richard Femell of East Smithfield, London, blacksmith.   Bound to Robert Cox for 7 years in Virginia.   Oct. 16, 1684.
                                                                                      14/33

FENN, Thomas, carpenter.   Bound to John Richards for 4 years in Nevis. Age 22.   Jan. 15, 1684.   14/123

FENNELL, Richard.   Son of Richard Fennell of Epsham (Epsom), Surrey, blacksmith, deced.   Bound to Thomas Tench for 8 years in Maryland. Aug. 4, 1684.   13

FENTON, Mary.   Going to Barbadoes.   Nov. 12, 1690.   15/20a

FERNANDES, Abraham.   Going to Jamaica.   Oct. 14, 1691.   15/53

FICH, Mary.   Daughter of Robert Fich of Goswell Street, St. Giles,
Cripplegate, London, weaver, deced.   Bound to Henry Turner for 4 years
in Virginia.   Oct. 6, 1684.   14/26

FINCH, Margaret, spinster.   Bound to James Finch for 7 years in Pensilvania.
Age 17.   April 10, 1686.   Witnesses William Burch and William Mackrith.
                                                                                   14/600

FISHER, Abell, blacksmith.   Bound to John Shaw for 4 years in Jamaica.
Age 22.   March 11, 1684.   14/181

FLEET, Elizabeth.   Daughter of William Fleet, butcher, deced.   Bound to
William Lock for 4 years in Mount Serratt.   April 10, 1685.   14/217

FLETCHER, Elizabeth.   Daughter of John Fletcher of Drury Lane in St.
Giles, Middlesex.   Bound to Nathaniel Jones for 4 years in Jamaica.   Age
22 or thereabouts.   March 2, 1684.   14/167

FLEURIOTT, D. and J; BAULDRY, J. and E.; LE TORT.   All French
Protestants bound at the request of Jean du Mastre and Stephen Nognier or
Noguier, deacons of French Church in London.

FLEURIOTT, Daniel.   Son of Jean Fleuriott of London (q. v.).   Bound to
Marmaduke Larkin for 7 years in Maryland.   Age 15.   Aug. 4, 1685.
(Has brother also Jean Fleuriott.   Note they did not go to same colony as
parents.   See above).   14/354

FLEURIOTT, Jean.   Son of Jean Fleuriott (q. v.).   Bound to Marmaduke
Larkin for 8 years in Maryland.   Age 14.   Aug. 4, 1685   14/354

FLEURIOTT, Jean of London, labourer and Louise his wife.   Bound to
Marmaduke Larkin for 4 years in Jamaica.   Aug. 3, 1685.   (Father of
Jean and Daniel above.   See ANBIER).   14/353

FLEURIOTT, Louise.   See FLEURIOTT, Jean.   Also see ANBIER.

FLICKNELL, Rebecka.   Daughter of Henry Flicknell of London, taylor,
deced.   Bound to Richard Cornwallis for 5 years in Virginia.   Age 15.

Dec. 30, 1685.   Witness Rebecka Bond, her mother.   14/488

FORRESTER, Dorothy, unmarried.   Bound to Charles Richards for 4 years
in Jamaica.   Age 23.   March 29, 1686.   14/552

FORT, John.   Son of Richard Fort, Aldgate, Middlesex, husbandman, deced.
Bound to Elizabeth Norris for 4 years in Maryland.   Witness Jane Fort, his
mother.   Aug. 27, 1685.   14/382

FOSTER, Elizabeth.   Bound to John Shaw for 4 years in Virginia.   Age 21.
March 10, 1684.   14/179

FOSTER, Leonard.   A poor boy.   Bound to Edward Peirce for 9 years in
Antego.   Consent of Churchwardens of parish of St. Leonard, Foster Lane,
Richard Broome and John Cruttall.   March 5, 1685.   Probably a foundling,
judging by his name and the name of the parish).   14/537

FOSTER, Mary.   Daughter of Robert Foster of Norwich, maltster, deced.
Bound to Roger Newman for 5 years in Maryland.   Age 19.   Aug. 11, 1685.
                                                                     14/365

FOWKES, Richard.   Bound to George Philipps for 4 years in Jamaica.   Age
32.   Aug. 28, 1685.   Witness Richard Thomas of White Chapple.   14/384

FOX, George.   Son of James Fox of Tividale (Teviotdale) in the Kingdom
of Scotland, blacksmith, deced.   Bound to William Tyleby for 4 years in
Jamaica.   Age 35.   Jan. 28, 1685.   14/506

FOX, Thomas.   Son of John Fox of Berry Pomeyroy, Devonshire, butcher,
deced.   Bound to John Walters for 5 years in Virginia.   Sept. 8, 1684.
                                                                     14/3

FRANKLIN, Thomas.   Son of Abraham Franklin of Dunnings Ally, Billings-
gate Street, London, weaver.   Bound to Thomas Nicchols for 4 years in
Jamaica.   Feb. 27, 1684.   14/165

FRANKLYN, Martin.   Son of Richard Franklyn, late of Kilburne, Middlesex,
husbandman.   Bound to Peter Barton for 4 years in Virginia.   Oct. 2,
1684.   14/23

FRAY, William.   Son of Thomas Fray of Canterbury, deced.   Bound to
Thomas Tench for 4 years in Maryland.   July 28, 1684.   13

FRAZER, Margaret, of St. Martins in the Fields, Middlesex. Bound to Robert Barrington for 4 years in the West Indies. Jan. 7, 1684.   14/114

FREEZE, John. Bound to John Williams for 4 years in Barbadoes. March 30, 1685.   14/203

FREMANTEEL, Ahazuemes of Old Baylee, London, printer. Bound to Thomas Meach for 4 years in New Yorke. June 16, 1686. Witness Bartholemew Sprint of the Old Change, printer.   14

FULLAM, Francis. Son of Jacob Fullam of Dublin, Ireland, taylor, deced. Bound to Peter Noyce for 8 years in New England. May 30, 1684.   13

FULLERTON, Alexander. Bound to John Haslewood for 4 years in Virginia. July 14, 1684.   13

FULLIGAR, Ann. Daughter of Matthias Fulligar, alias Dominee of Upchurch, Kent. Bound to John Triggs for 4 years in Virginia. Nov. 10, 1684. 14/55

FULSTONE, John. Bound to John Prim for 7 years in Virginia. Sept. 9, 1684.   14/5

G

GALE, John.   Going to Port Royal, Jamaica, to his father.   Nov. 11, 1690.
15/20

GARDINER, John.   Bound to Richard Pateson for 4 years in Jamaica.   Age 25.
Nov. 18, 1684.   14/67

GARDNER, Thomas of Northampton.   Bound to Robert Cox for 4 years in
Virginia.   Oct. 17, 1684.   14/33

GARNET, James.   Son of John Garnet of parish of St. (Botolph) Without
Bishopsgate (London), deced.   Bound to Richard Solley for 7 years in
Maryland.   July 31, 1685.   14/350

GARNETT, Sarah.   Bound to Samuel Claphamson for 4 years in Virginia.
Age 20.   Sept. 18, 1685.   14/405

GARRETT, Joseph of London.   Bound to Thomas Chinery for 4 years in
Jamaica.   June 8, 1685.   14/275

GARTH, Richard.   Son of Avery Garth of Hangham (Ingham?), Lincolne,
gentleman, deced.   Bound to William Kirkham for 4 years in Barbadoes.
Age 19.   Nov. 30, 1685.   14/465

GAY, Richard.   Bound to Thomas Gay, Esq. for 4 years in Jamaica.   Age
24.   June 5, 1685.   14/273

GENTLEMAN, Thomas.   Son of Evers Gentleman, deced.   Bound to
Richard Smith for 7 years in Maryland.   July 27, 1685.   14/343

GENTLEMAN, William, son of William Gentleman of Chareing Cross (London), porter, deced.   "Being pilfering boys that lie day and night in the marketts and streets of this city, and haveing noe friends or relations to take care or provide for them, came before his lordship and of their owne free accord bound themselves severally by indentures to John Lightfoot, planter, lodging at Mr. Edmond Lightfoot's without Newgate, to serve him in Virginia..."   Term: 15 years.   July 4, 1684.   (See William JONES, Thos. HATHORNE and also Henry HARDING, etc).   13

GEORGE, Richard. Son of Richard George, Debtford (London). gardner, deced. Bound to John Haslewood for 10 years in Virginia. July 4, 1684. 13

GIBBLE, Robert. Son of William Gibble, late of Exeter Street, Shawditch, Middlesex, gentleman, deced. Bound to Rene Drignion for 4 years in Pensilvania. May 1, 1684. 13

GIBBONS, John. Son of Henry Gibbons, late of Mells in Somerset, mealman, deced. Bound to John Wynn for 6 years in Virginia. Sept. 26, 1684. 14/19

GIBBS, Francis, of London, labourer. Bound to Francis and Elizabeth Edwin for 5 years in Virginia. Sept. 30, 1684. 14/22

GIBBS, Sarah. Daughter of Nicholas Gibbs of Bishopsgate, silkweaver, deced. Bound to Thomas Meache for 4 years in New Yorke. Age 18. June 17, 1686. Witness Amy Gibbs, widow, her mother. 14

GILBERT, Mary. Daughter of Mary Gilbert of Long Lane in Smithfields (London). Bound to John Haines and Elizabeth his wife for 5 years in Maryland. July 24, 1685. 14/339

GILES, William. Son of John Giles of Mitcham in Surrey "with the consent of Mary Giles, his mother". Bound to Benjamin Goodin for 6 years in Jamaica. Jan. 7, 1684. 14/114

GILFORD, Robert. Bound to George Pye for 4 years (No destination). Jan. 26, 1682. 13

GLASSE, James. Port Royal, Jamaica. Nov. 11, 1690. 15/20

GLASSEBROOKE, Roger. Bound to John Marden for 4 years in Virginia. Age 27. Aug. 25, 1685. "Was lately discharged as a soldier". 14/379

GLOVER, Blanch. Bound to Marmaduke Larkin for 4 years in Maryland. July 23, 1685. Witness Hester Whittaker, joyner's wife, Strand (London). 14/338

GODARD, Stephen. Son of Stephen Godard of Shoe Lane, London, deced. "By consent of his mother Elizabeth". Bound to Robert Shanks for 4 years in Jamaica. Dec. 9, 1684. 14/93

GODDARD, Mr.   Pass to Barbadoes.   Nov. 10, 1690.   15/19

GODFREY, John.   Bound to William Nash for 4 years in Jamaica.   Age 23.
Sept. 23, 1685.   Witness the said William Nash, his cousin.   14/413

GODFREY, John and his wife and kinswoman.   To Jamaica.   Nov. 10, 1690.
                                                                    15/19a

GODFREY, William.   To St. Christophers.   Nov. 12, 1690.   15/21

GOFF, Anthony of London, vintner.   Bound to Francis Mingham for 4 years
in Jamaica.   Age 27.   Nov. 23, 1685.   14/459

GOFFE, John.   Son of Roger Goffe late of St. Pauls, Shadwell, butcher,
deced.   Bound to Edmond Sandiford for 5 years in Barbadoes.   Aug. 22,
1685.   Witnesses Bennett Pickford, his mother and William Pickford, his
father-in-law.   14/375

GOLD, Samuel, son of John Gold, London, cabinetmaker, deced.   Bound
to George Doughty for 5 years in Virginia.   Sept. 29, 1685.   14/420

GOLDING, Daniel, taylor.   No mother living but father lives in Jamaica.
Bound to Thomas Sawell for 4 years in Jamaica.   Age 18.   June 12, 1685.
Witness Isaac Johnson.   14/277

GOODIN, Anne.   Daughter of Thomas Goodin of Shawditch, Middlesex.
Bound to Richard Anniver for 4 years in Jamaica.   Nov. 13, 1684.   14/58

GOULD, Ursula.   To Barbadoes.   Nov. 15, 1690.   15/23

GRAINGER or GRANGER, Mary, daughter of Anne Dawson of Princes
Street, Leicester Gdn., widow.   Bound to William Tayleby for 4 years in
Jamaica.   Age 28.   Dec. 2, 1685   14/467

GRANT, John.   Son of John Grant, marriner.   Bound to John Lightfoot for
10 years in Virginia.   July 25, 1684.   13

GRANT, Ralph of Rochester, Kent, blacksmith.   Bound to William Dockwra
for 4 years in East New Jersey.   Age 22.   March 17, 1684.   14/189

GRAVELL, John.   Bound to Francis Hanson for 5 years in Jamaica.   Age 16.
Nov. 27, 1685.   14/463

GRAY, Henry.   Son of William Gray of Durham.   Bound to Robert Thorne for 4 years in Virginia.   Age 20.   Aug 20, 1685.   Witness Jeffrey Barnes, who had known him for a considerable time in London.   14/374

GRAY, John.   Son of John Gray, late of St. Martin in the Fields, Middlesex, taylor, deced.   Bound to Francis and Elizabeth Edwin for 14 years in Virginia.   Sept. 29, 1684.   14/22

GRAY, Mary, widow.   To Barbadoes.   Nov. 10, 1690.   15/19a

GREATOREX, Katherine.   See Edward PATTISON.

GREATOREX, Ralph.   See Edward PATTISON.

GREEN, Elizabeth, spinster.   Bound to John Rudds for 4 years in Virginia.   Age 16.   Sept. 22, 1685.   Witness Peter Green of Minories, London, her father.   14/410

GREEN, William.   Bound to John Guyet for 7 years in Maryland.   Age 16.   Oct. 22, 1685.   Witness Mary Phillipps.   14/437

GREENAWAY, Bridget.   Daughter of William Greenaway, late waterman, deced.   Bound to Francis and Elizabeth Edwin for 7 years in Virginia.   Oct. 1, 1684.   14/23

GREENAWAY, Mary.   Daughter of Henry Greenaway, gentleman, of St. Pauls Wharfe, London, deced.   Bound to Christopher Prissicke for 4 years in Barbadoes.   Witness Rebeccah Session, her cozen.   March 31, 1686.
                                                          14/555

GREENWOOD, Rachell.   Bound to John Lightfoot for 5 years in Virginia.   July 14, 1684.   13

GRIFFIN, Charles.   Son of Geo. Griffin of Shipston upon Stower (Stour), Worcestershire.   Bound to Geo. Phillipps for 4 years in Jamaica.   April 28, 1685.   14/227

GRIFFIN, Richard.   Son of Richard Griffin, late of Whitechappel (London), seaman, deced.   Bound to Michaell Petry and Thomas Laine for 10 years in Virginia.   July 22, 1684.   13

GRIGGS, Thomas.   Son of Thomas Griggs of Golding Lane, London, joyner,

deced.   Bound to Joel Kent for 7 years in Virginia.   Oct. 12, 1685.
Witness Mary Griggs, his sister.   Oct. 12, 1685.   14/430

GRIMES, Robert.   Bound to Thomas Thatcher for 4 years in Jamaica.
Age 23.   Oct. 23, 1684.   14/41

GUALTER, Thomas.   Bound to John Moorhead for 4 years in Jamaica.
Age 22.   May 5, 1685.   Witness John Rogers of Shoe Lane, cooper.   14/237

GUESHARD, Samuel.   See Edward CALIGNON.

GUFFY, John.   Son of Francis Guffy of the French Almeshouses in Spittlefeilds.   Bound to Robert Burman for 5 years in Maryland.   July 21, 1685.
(See Jacob WILBOW)   14/333

GUILLE, Anna.   Wife of Isaac GUILLE, q. v.   Bound for 4 years.

GUILLE, Isaac, his wife Anna and children Magdalene, John, Peter, Stephen
and Joseph.   All bound to Augustine Boullay in Virginia.   Sept. 16, 1685.
                                                                    14/404

GUILLE, Isaac.   Bound for 4 years.   See above.

GUILLE, John.   Bound for 5 years.   See Isaac GUILLE.

GUILLE, Joseph.   Bound for 11 years.   See Isaac GUILLE.

GUILLE. Magdalene.   Bound for 5 years.   See Isaac GUILLE.

GUILLE, Stephen.   Bound for 7 years.   See Isaac GUILLE.

GUN, Mary of London, spinster.   Bound to James and Margaret Skinner for
4 years in Jamaica.   Age 18.   Sept. 29, 1685.   Witness John Gun, her
brother.   14/420

GURNEY, Lott.   See Anne SIMONDS.

H

HACKLEY, Sarah. Sister of Thomas Hackley of St. Clements Lane, London, barber. Bound to Thomas Jackson for 4 years in Virginia. Sept. 16, 1685.   14/402

HACON, Samuel. Bound to William Flood for 8 years in Jamaica. Age 12. Sept. 21, 1685. Witness Mary Porter his sister.   14/409

HAGAR, William. Son of Robert Hagar, Bishopsgate Street (London), weaver, deced. Bound to John Haslewood for 10 years in Virginia. July 4, 1684. (See Henry HARDING).   13

HAITE, Mary. Daughter of John Haite of Bozett (Bozeat), Northampton, labourer, deced. Bound to John Haslewood for 4 years in Virginia. Age 18. June 18, 1686.   14

HALL, Katherina. Bound to Robert Burrman for 4 years in Maryland. July 24, 1685. Witness Sarah Hall, her aunt.   14/338

HALL, Mary, of Southwarke. Bound to Gabriell Bonner for 6 years in Virginia. Age 15. Jan. 20, 1685. Witness Richard Prosgrove, her brother.   14/500

HALL, Mathew. See Elizabeth HUMES.

HALL, Richard. "His mother and father being dead". Bound to John Lightfoot for 9 years in Virginia. June 23, 1684. Witness Elizabeth Chidley, his grandmother.   13

HALL, Robert, Mr. Merchant. Pass to Barbadoes. Feb. 6, 1690. 15/28

HALL, William. Son of Alexander Hall, Mich Badde (Probably Great Baddow), Essex, deced. Bound to Phillip Gower for 9 years in Jamaica. March 26, 1684.   14/196

HALLIDAY, Joseph of Sunderland in the bishopricke of Durham. Bound to Edward Hill for 4 years in Barbadoes. June 15, 1686.   14

HAMDEN, Elizabeth, of London, widow.   Bound to John Wynn for 5 years in Virginia.   Oct. 1, 1684.   14/23

HAMOND, Benjamin.   Bound to William Holliday for 5 years in Maryland. Age 26.   Aug. 24, 1685.   14/378

HANCOCK, William.   Son of Walter Hancock of Mark, Somerset, farryer, deced.   Bound to John Williams for 4 years in Barbadoes.   Age 23. April 24, 1685.   Unmarried.   14/223

HANCOCKS, Thomas.   Son of John Hancocks of Worcester (city), barge-man.   Bound to Thomas Warren for 7 years in Maryland.   July 21, 1684.
                                                                        13

HANDS, Katherine.   "Being a stout young woman".   Bound to Thomas Baylee for 5 years in Carolina.   Age 25.   Dec. 7, 1685.   Witness Diana Roman.   14/473

HANLEY, Thomas.   Son of Thomas Hanley of St. Giles in the Feilds (Middlesex).   Bound to John and Elizabeth Haines for 4 years in Maryland. July 24, 1685.   Witness Dennis Hanley, his mother.   14/339

HANSON, John.   To Maryland.   June 24, 1691.   15/40

HARBOTTLE, John.   Son of John Harbottle of St. Giles in the Fields, (Middlesex).   Bound to Roger Newman for 7 years in Maryland.   Aug. 11, 1685.   14/363

HARDING, Anthony.   Bound to James Harding for 4 years in Jamaica. Nov. 10, 1685.   Witness Simon Webb, Goodmans Yard (London?), cutler, his cozen.   14/445

HARDING, Henry.   Also Dukesell BROWNE, Richard GEORGE, Robert IPEY, William HAGAR.   Same entry and all the same details "Being pilfering boys," etc. as William GENTLEMAN, q. v.   Bound to John Haslewood for 10 years in Virginia.   July 4, 1684.   13

HARDY, Mary, spinster.   Bound to John Triggs for 4 years in Virginia. Age 23.   Nov. 21, 1684.   14/70

HARDY, Thomas.   Bound to John Dikes for 4 years in Barbadoes.   Age22. April 8, 1685.   14/214.

HARGRAVE, Edward.   Bound to George Buckerton for 4 years (No destination) July 4, 1683.   Witness Mr. Philipps, a brazier, near Holbourne Hill.   13

HARMAN, John and Mathias, his brother.   Sons of William Harman of Hanslipp, near Strong Stratford (Hanslope, near Stony Stratford), Bucking- hamshire, labourer.   Bound to John Glover for 4 years in Barbadoes. July 14, 1685.   14/326

HARMAN, Mathias.   See John HARMAN.

HARRIS, James, glass bottle maker.   Bound to Joseph Martin for 4 years in Pensilvania "to serve them (i. e. the Free Society of Traders in Pennsylvania of which Joseph Martin was chief agent) there as a glass bottle maker for 4 yeares after his arriveall by indentures dated the 3oth of August last". Sept. 4, 1684.   13

HARRIS, Jane.   Daughter of Elizabeth, the wife of Abraham Medcalfe of St. Thomas Southwark, by their consent.   Bound to Henry Hawkins for 10 years in Maryland.   August 10, 1685.   14/362

HARRIS, Thomas.   Son of John Harris of Bristow (Bristol?), distiller, deced. Bound to Ernesto Keckerbart for 4 years in Virginia.   Age 28.   Aug. 11, 1685.   14/364

HARRIS, Thomas "An Indian, aged 16 years or thereabouts, and Mary HEWETT, daughter of Thomas Hewett, late of Nottingham, taylor, deced. Age 19 years or thereabouts, single woman.   Both came voluntarily with Nathaneill Willett, turnkey of Bridewell (prison) within the city of West- minster, bound to Richard Ally of Westminster, gent. to serve him or his assignes in West Indies for 4 years apiece".   Feb. 23, 1685.   14/529

HARRIS, William.   To Barbadoes.   With Katherine and Mary PEGSON, Robert CUNYNGHAM and a negro boy, his servants.   Nov. 13, 1690.
                                                                      15/21a

HARRISON, Easter, widow.   Daughter of Elias Shie of Wapping, shipwright. Bound to Matthew Trim for 4 years in Virginia.   Nov. 10, 1684.   14/55

HARRISON, Edward.   Bound to John Dikes for 4 years in Barbadoes.   Age 30. April 7, 1685.   14/214

HARRISON, John.   Son of Sidrick Harrison, Blewe Coates Feild, Ratcliffe,

(London), mariner, deced. Bound to Thomas Tench for 9 years in Maryland.
July 25, 1684. 13

HARRISON, Jubily. Daughter of William Harrison, late of Shrewsbury,
Shropshire, deced. Bound to Emanuell Winsor for 4 years in New Yorke.
Age 22. March 25, 1685. 14/195

HARRISON, Mary, widow. Bound to William Flood for 4 years in Jamaica.
Age 26. Oct. 24, 1684. 14/42

HARTLEY, Joshua. Bound to John Seaman for 4 years in Maryland. Age
21. July 27, 1685. (See also John JONES and George CLARLY). 14/344

HARTWELL, Francis. Bound to Thomas Price for 4 years in Jamaica.
Age 23. April 27, 1686. Witness Thomas Hartwell of Covent Garden, his
brother. 14/616

HARVEY, Symon. Son of Symon Harvey of Oxford, cordwainer. Bound
to Robert Shanks for 8 years in Jamaica. Oct. 9, 1684. 14/28

HATHORNE, Thomas. Son of Thomas Hathorne, Crosse Lane, near
Holbourne, (London), joyner, deced. Bound to John Lightfoot for 10 years
in Virginia. July 4, 1684. (See William GENTLEMAN). 13

HAWKINS, Thomas of Abington (don), Berkshire. Bound to John Bunce
for 4 years in Pensilvania. April 16, 1686. 14/602

HAYKINS, Mary. Daughter of William Haykins, late of Norwich. Bound
to Robert Shanks for 4 years in Virginia. Sept. 30, 1684. (Same entry
as Martha RICHARDSON). 14/22

HAYNE, Anne, of Norfolk. now of London, spinster. Bound to John Robinson for 4 years in Jamaica. Age 26. May 1, 1686. Witness Phillipp
Atkins. (Same entry as M. DELAMOTT). 14/621

HAYWARD, Edward. Son of John Hayward. Bound to William Cherrey
for 7 years in Barbadoes. Feb. 7, 1682. 13

HEATH, Elias. Pass to Boston, New England, the place of his abode,
embarking at Portsmouth. Oct. 18, 1690. 15/18a

HEATHCOTE, Mr. and three others. A Pass to travel to Portsmouth and thence to New Yorke.   Oct. 13, 1690.   15/18

HEATHCOATE, John.   Pass granted to "travel to Gravesend to take his
passage on board Capt. Wm. Mingham, for Jamaica. " Witness Mr. Barron
of Coalman Street.   July 3, 1685.   14/309

HELLIER, Thomas.   Son of Robert Hellier of Chudley (Chudleigh), Devon,
limeburner.   Bound to David Lockwood for 4 years in Jamaica. Nov. 8,
1684.   14/52

HENRICK, Joachim.   Bound to Jane Haynes for 4 years in Jamaica.   Age
24.   Dec. 16, 1685.   14/480

HERVE or HERVÉ, Thomas of London, labourer.   A Frenchman.   Bound to
Marmaduke Larkin for 4 years in Maryland.   Age 19.   Aug. 4, 1685.
                                                            14/355

HESCOCK, Easter, widow.   Daughter of Richard Pemberton, deced.
Bound to Richard Phillipps for 5 years in Maryland.   Age 18.   July 23,
1685.   Witness Anne Pemberton of St. Annes Lane, Aldersgate, her sister.
                                                            14/337

HEWETT, Mary.   See Thomas HARRIS.

HICKMAN, Edward.   Son of Edward Hickman, late of Newport Pannell
(Pagnall) in Buckinghamshire, cornchandler.   Bound to Thomas Newbold
for 5 years in Maryland.   Age 21.   Aug. 21, 1685.   Witness John Willson
his father-in-law.   14/375

HICKMAN, Elizabeth.   Daughter of William Hickman of London, porter.
Bound to John and Elizabeth Haynes for 7 years in Maryland.   July 27, 1685.
                                                            14/344

HILL, Caleb.   Bound to Thomas Adams for 4 years in Port Royall, Jamaica.
May 21, 1684.   13

HILL, Jane.   Bound to Samuel Sleigh for 7 years in Jamaica.   Age 15.
April 16, 1686.   Witness Katherine, her mother.   14/601

HILL, Richard.   Son of Nathan Hill of St. Giles, Criplegate, London,
silkstockwinder,   deced.   Bound to Roger Edwards for 8 years in Jamaica.
May 30, 1684.   13

HILL, Sarah. Daughter of Isabell Hill of Highgate. Bound to Samuell Broadway for 4 years in Jamaica. May 18, 1685.   14/255

HILL, William of London. Bound to John Pym for 4 years in Jamaica. Age 20. July 9, 1685. Consent of John Hill, his brother, of Fenchurch Street (London).   14/321

HILLS, Margaret. Daughter of Thomas Hills of Sawston in Cambridgeshire, deced. Bound to Nicholas Richardson for 4 years in Jamaica. Oct. 11, 1684.   14/29

HILTON, Margaret of London, spinster. Bound to Thomas Ridder for 4 years in Maryland. Age 28. Sept. 3, 1685. Witness Katherine Ridder, wife of Thomas.   14/389

HOCROFT, Thomas. Bound to Christopher Robinson for 9 years in Virginia. Aug. 18, 1684.   13

HODGES, Elizabeth of London, spinster. Bound to John Oakly for 4 years in Maryland. Age 21. Nov. 26, 1684.   14/74

HODGES, Samuel. Son of John Hodges, deced. Bound to John Drapentier for 8 years in Virginia. Age 12. Sept. 30, 1685.   14/420

HOGG, Ambrose of Urcester(Uttoxeter ?), Staffordshire, labourer. Bound to Robert Burman for 4 years in Maryland. Age 20. Aug. 5, 1685. "Being lately a souldier in His Majesties army against the rebells and discharged by his captaine." (Ref. to Duke of Monmouth's Rebellion).   14/355

HOLDEN, Edward. Son of Edward Holden of Minories, London, customhouse officer. Bound to Geo. Phillipps for 4 years in Jamaica. Age 16. April 24, 1685.   14/223

HOLLOWAY, Richard of London, labourer. Bound to Thomas Green for 4 years in Jamaica. Oct. 31, 1684.   14/47

HOLLYMON, Martha, spinster. Bound to John Hanforde for 5 years in Virginia. Aug. 21, 1684.   13

HOLMES, Henry. Son of Henry Holmes of Shawditch, deced. "Upon affirmation of the said John Dixon and Mary his wife..." (See T. BAGLEY). Bound to Philip Gore for 7 years in Jamaica. April 29, 1685.   14/228

HOLTON, Isaak.   Son of Richard Holton, late of London, linen draper,
deced.   Bound to Robert White, his father-in-law for 5 years in Barbadoes.
Age 16.   Sept. 9, 1685.   Witness Mary White, his mother.   14/393

HONNOTT, John and Martha, his wife of Alresford, Hampshire, sawyer.
Bound to James Streater for 4 years in Pensilvania.   April 2, 1686.   14/557

HONNOTT, Martha.   See John HONNOTT.

HOOPER, William, labourer.   Son of William Hooper of Taunton, Somerset.   Bound to John Langley for 5 years in Barbadoes.   Age 21.   March 18,
1684.   "Neither father nor mother living".   14/191

HORFFORD, Byworth of London, labourer.   Bound to Christopher Byerley for
4 years in Carolina.   Feb. 19, 1685.   14/525

HUDSON, Nathaniel.   Bound to Elizabeth Wicks for 5 years in Virginia.
Age 25.   Oct. 24, 1685.   Witness Mary Wheeler of Holborn Bridge, his
sister, widow.   14/438

HUGGINS, Michael.   Servant of Richard Veysey, q.v.

HUGHES, Mary of London, spinster.   Bound to Matthew Trim for 5 years
in Virginia.   Nov. 19, 1684.   14/68

HUMES, Elizabeth.   Bound to Andrew Hardy of Virginia, planter for 4
years.   Jan. 4, 1682.   Also on same entry, but bound for 5 years: William
DAVIS, Mathew HALL, Thomas WAKELY.   13

HUNT, Mary, spinster.   Bound to John Lloyd for 4 years in Nevis.   Age 17.
Oct. 24, 1685.   Witness Samuel Upshaw, her brother, of Southwarke,
painter.   14/438

HUTTON, Mary.   Bound to John Robinson for 4 years in Jamaica.   Age 19.
May 1, 1686.   Witness Mary Trevailer.   (See Rebeccah ROBINSON).   14/621

HYFIELD, John.   Bound to Thomas Cradock for 4 years in Virginia.   Age 17.
Nov. 18, 1685.   Witness Rebecca Noakes, his mother, wife of William
Noakes, Whitechapple (London).   14/453

I

INGE, Richard.   See Peter BECKFORD.

INGULL, William, of Absrowdin (Roding Abbess), Essex, husbandman.
Bound to Barnaby Cater for 4 years in Barbadoes.   Age 28.   Not married.
April 28, 1685.   14/227

IPEY, Robert.   Son of Robert Ipey, Rosemary Lane, deced.   Bound to
John Haslewood for 10 years in Virginia.   July 4, 1684.   (See Henry
HARDING).   13

J

JACKMAN, Elizabeth. Daughter of John Jackman of Oakley (Ockley?) Surrey, husbandman, deced. Bound to Thomas Davies for 4 years in Barbadoes. June 17, 1686. (Same entry as Elizabeth DAVIES). 14

JACKSON, William. Bound to John Fleming for 4 years in Jamaica. Jan. 26, 1682. 13

JAMES, Edward. Son of William James of Redriffe (Rotherhithe), Surrey. Bound to Thomas Nicholls for 8 years in America. Witness William Partridge, barber, his half brother. March 29, 1686. 14/552

JAMES, Elizabeth of Wapping, spinster. Bound to Jeremiah Resler for 5 years in Maryland. Aug. 31, 1685. 14/387

JAMES, Mary. Daughter of Edward James of Chillington, Somerset. Bound to Richard Cornwallis for 5 years in Virginia. Oct. 9, 1684. 14/29

JAMES, Moses. Bound to William Holliday for 5 years in Maryland. Age 21. Aug. 24, 1685. 14/378

JAMES, Simon. Son of Thomas James of Chepstow in Monmouth, husbandman, deced. Bound to Phillip Gower for 4 years in Jamaica. Age 40. May 22, 1685. 14/260

JANE, Mary. To Barbadoes. Nov. 15, 1690. 15/23

JEANE, William. Bound to Robert Shancks for 4 years in Jamaica. Age 22. Dec. 18, 1684. 14/99

JEFFREY, Thomas. Son of John Jeffrey, ragman. Bound to David Browne for 7 years in Virginia. Oct. 9, 1684. 14/28

JENKINS, John. Bound to Gilbert Ashley for 6 years in the island of New Providence in America. Oct. 22, 1683. 13

JENNINGS, Josephus. Son of Barthew. Jennings, late of Southwarke, deced. Bound to John Tanner for 8 years in Maryland. Witness Joane Jennings, his mother. Aug. 28, 1685. 14/383

JERMAN, Anthony.   Son of John Jerman, taylor, Hatton Garden, Middlesex.
Bound to Gabriell Bonner for 4 years in Virginia.   Age 17.   Jan. 2, 1685.
14/489

JEWELL, Mary.   Daughter of Joseph Jewell, deced.   Bound to Hugh Gardner
for 4 years in Virginia.   Aug. 27, 1684.   13

JOHNSON, Elizabeth.   To Maryland.   June 24, 1691.   15/40

JOHNSON, Elizabeth, wife of Solomon Johnson.   Bound to Hugh Gardner
for 4 years in Virginia.   Aug. 27, 1684.   13

JOHNSON, John, of Cottnam (Cottenham), Cambridge, carpenter.   Bound
to Robert Shanks for 4 years in Jamaica.   Age 30.   Dec. 22, 1684.   14/104

JOHNSON, Joseph of Paddington (Piddington), Oxfordshire.   Bound to John
Bayne for 4 years in Maryland.   Age 30.   Dec. 5, 1685.   14/469

JOHNSON, Solomon and Elizabeth his wife.   Bound to Hugh Gardner for
4 years in Virginia. Aug. 27, 1684.   13

JOHNSON, Thomas.   Son of Thomas Johnson of Bolston (Boyleston?) in
Derbyshire.   Bound to Phillipp Gower for 4 years in Jamaica.   Age 26.
May 28, 1685. Witness Marmaduke Procter   14/264

JOHNSON, William.   Son of William Johnson, Abergany (Abergavenny),
Monmouthshire, deced.   Bound to Christopher Jefferson for 4 years in St.
Christophers.   Age 30.   Feb. 23, 1685.   14/529

JONES, Alice.   Bound to Gilbert Ashley for 4 years in New Providence.
Oct. 22, 1683.   13

JONES, Elizabeth, spinster.   Bound to Robert Eldridge for 4 years in
Virginia.   Age 17.   Jan. 11, 1685.   14/495

JONES, Griffith.   Son of David Jones, late of Coychurch, Glamorgan,
yeoman, deced.   Bound to William Bonniface for 4 years in Jamaica.
Age 19.   May 19, 1685. Witness John Burton, St. Mary Magdalene,
Bermondsey, "knew him for many years".   14/258

JONES, James.   Bound to Phillipp Quinton for 4 years in Barbadoes.   Age 23.
Feb. 9, 1685.   14/517

JONES, Jane.   Daughter of John Jones, late of Derby Castle, Derbyshire, glover, deced.   Bound to William Lawes for 4 years in Jamaica.   April 22, 1685.
14/221

JONES, John.   Son of John Jones, late of Mile End in Middlesex.   Bound to Alexander Pollington for 6 years in Antigua.   Age 17.   Dec. 1, 1684.
14/82

JONES, John.   Bound to John Seaman for 4 years in Maryland.   Age 22. July 27, 1685.   With Joshua HARTLEY and George CLARLY "All 3 brought by the turnkey of New Prison, haveing been prisoners there and lyeing onely for their fees".
14/344

JONES, Joseph of London, miller.   Bound to William Goodman for 4 years in Jamaica.   Age 22.   June 8, 1685.   "By the information of Thomas Slade in Rosemary Lane in East Smithfield, blacksmith, that he had knowne the aforesaid about a quarter of a year last in London and knew him when he lived in Monmouth Bridge within four miles of Shousberry (?) and that he then had but a mother alive... "
14/275

JONES, Mary.   Daughter of Robert Jones near Ruthen (Ruthin), Denbighshire, Wales, mason.   Bound to John Tanner for 4 years in Virginia.   Age 28. Aug. 10, 1685.
14/362

JONES, Sarah.   Bound to Philip Holland for 6 years in Maryland.   July 21, 1685.   "Upon the recomendation of Susannah Marshall of White Fryers, her nurse. "
14/334

JONES, Thomas.   Son of Richard Jones of Monmouth (city), husbandman, deced.   Bound to Thomas Austin for 4 years in Antego in West Indies. Age 22.   Dec. 2, 1685.
14/466

JONES, William.   Son of William Jones of Whitechappell, taylor, deced. Bound to John Lightfoot for 12 years in Virginia.   July 4, 1684.   (See William Gentleman).
13

JOVERELL, John, of City of Gloucester.   Glass bottle maker.   Bound to Joseph Martin for 4 years in Pensilvania.   Feb. 8, 1683.
13

JUDKIN, Elizabeth, spinster.   Bound to Anna Keckerbert for 7 years in Virginia.   Age 14.   Oct. 22, 1685.   Witness William Judkin of Northumberland Alley, Fenchurch St (London), shoemaker, her father.
14/437

K

KAHAN, John.   Bound to Richard Pateson for 4 years in Jamaica.   Age 22.
Nov. 21, 1684.   Footnote: At Deale.   14/70

KAINE, Anthony.   Son of Charles Kaine, late of Southwarke.   Bound to
Richard Stephens for 7 years in Virginia.   Age 13.   July 17, 1685.   Consent
of Judith Kaine, his mother.   14/329

KENNEDY, Michael.   Bound to John Pym for 4 years in Jamaica.   Age 20.
April 8, 1686.   Witness Elizabeth Jones, widow.   14/559

KENT, Abraham.   Bound to William Martin for 4 years in Jamaica.   Dec.
20, 1684.   14/103

KEWELL, Sarah.   Daughter of Thomas Kewell, late of Susson (Sutton?)
in Sussex, yeoman, deced.   Bound to Thomas Allon or Allen for 5 years
in Virginia.   July 16, 1685.   Witness Elizabeth Hall.   14/328

KIBBLEWIGHT, Elizabeth, spinster.   Bound to John Mapleston for 4 years
in Jamaica.   Age 25.   May 6, 1685.   Witness Thomas Prine, Minories
(London), shoemaker.   14/240

KILLINGWORTH, Edward.   To Maryland.   June 24, 1691.   15/40

KING, Dorcas.   See Peter BECKFORD.

KNEWSTUBB, William.   Bound to John Brookes for 4 years in Jamaica.
Oct. 14, 1684.   14/30

KNIGHT, Patience of Southwark, Surrey, spinster.   Bound to Phillip
Clarke for 4 years in Maryland.   July 31, 1684.   13

L

LA CASTEEL, James.   Bound to James Williams for 4 years in Barbadoes.
Age 30.   May 7, 1686.   "Offering to make oath that he is a freeman and
unmarried".   (No indication that he is a French man in spite of the name;
and there is no mistaking the word freeman).   14

LAMBERT, Daniel.   Bound to John Williams for 4 years in Virginia.   Age
31.   March 12, 1684.   14/182

LANCASHIRE, Daniell.   Son of Robert Lancashire, Southwarke, collyer.
Bound to John Seaman for 7 years in Virginia.   July 19, 1684.   13

LANCASHIRE, Robert.   Brother of Daniell Lancashire, q. v.   Bound to
John Seaman for 5 years in Virginia.   July 19, 1684.   13

LATHORNE, Christopher.   Son of William Lathorne of Southwark, mapmaker,
deced.   Bound to Thomas Tench for 9 years in Maryland.   July 25, 1684.
                                                                          13

LAUGHTON, William.   Bound to Charles Richards for 4 years in Jamaica.
Age 24.   April 5, 1686.   14/558

LAWES, Elizabeth.   Bound to Gerrard Slye and Israel Morgan for 6 years
in Maryland.   May 16, 1683.   13

LAWRENCE, Richard.   Bound to John Robinson for 4 years in Jamaica.
Age 20.   May 6, 1686.   Witness Martin Wilkinson, his present master,
carpenter, of Clerkenwell (London).   14

LEDGER, Edward.   Bound to John Dikes for 4 years in Barbadoes.   Age 28.
April 6, 1685.   14/213

LE DOUX, Andre.   "A Frenchman, lately a souldier in the King's army but
dismissed by his captaine".   Bound to Marmaduke Larkin for 4 years in
Maryland.   Aug. 4, 1685.   (See Ambrose HOGG).   14/355

LE JEUN, Lucq, alias Lucq YOUNG, a native of Jersey (Channel Islands?)
Bound to John Netherway for 4 years in Nevis.   Jan. 23, 1684.   14/133

LE TORT, Jeanne.   Bound to Marmaduke Larkin for 4 years in Maryland.
Aug. 4, 1685. (See FLEURIOTT)   14/355

LETTEN, William.   Son of William Letten, late cooper of London.   Bound
to William Nash for 5 years in Jamaica.   Age 19.   May 13, 1685.   14/249

LEVERLAND, Charles.   Son of Lewin Leverland late of Oxford, deced.
Bound to Richard Cornwallis for 4 years in Virginia. Oct. 9, 1684.   14/29

LEWIS, Thomas of London, sawyer.   Bound to John Williams for 4 years in
Barbadoes.   Age 30.   March 21, 1684.   No wife or children.   14/193

LIGHTFOOT, Abraham.   Son of Thomas Lightfoot of Exeter, worsted comber.
Bound to Phillipp Gower for 4 years in Jamaica.   March 2, 1684.   14/167

LINDSEY, Mary, spinster.   Bound to Aronesto Keckerbecke for 4 years in
Virginia.   Of full age.   July 21, 1685.   14/334

LLOYD, Elizabeth.   Daughter of Jeremy Lloyd of St. Sepulcher, chimney
sweep.   Bound to Philip Clarke for 8 years in Maryland. July 28, 1684.   13

LLOYD, Francis.   Son of Thomas Lloyd, Parshaw (Pershore), Worcestershire,
gardener, deced.   Bound to Arnesto Kackerbart for 7 years in Virginia.
July 31, 1685.   Witness Mary Harley.   14/349

LOCKSON, Mary.   Daughter of John Lockson, late of Long Lane, pipemaker,
deced.   Bound to Robert Shanks for 4 years in Jamaica.   Oct. 9, 1684.
                                                                    14/28

LODGE, Henry, of Debtford.   Bound to Charles Richards for 3 years in
Jamaica.   Age 40.   March 29, 1686.   14/552

LOMSDALE, John.   Bound to David Lockwood for 4 years in Jamaica.
Nov. 19, 1684.   14/68

LONG, William.   Son of Humphrey Long, St. Martins in the Fields,
Middlesex, feltmaker, deced.   Bound to Francis Partis for 8 years in
Maryland.   Witness Ann Kittson, his mother. Aug. 18, 1685.   14/372

LOVE, Sarah.   To Jamaica.   June 22, 1691.   15/39a

LOVEDAY, Thomas, of Coxhill, (Coggeshall), Essex, gardener.   Bound to

John Richards for 4 years in Barbadoes. May 12, 1686. 14

LOWTHER, Thomas. Son of Thomas Lowther, late of Berwick-upon-Tweed. Bound to John Rose for 4 years in Jamaica. Dec. 31, 1684. 14/110

M

MABB, Arthur. Bound to Nicholas Parister for 4 years in Maryland. Age 20. Sept. 1, 1684. 13

MABLY, Sarah, spinster. Daughter of Thomas Mably. Bound to Robert Watkins for 4 years in Jamaica. Age 16. June 2, 1684. 13

MAC-GUIER, John. Bound to John Richard for 4 years in Maryland. Age 22. Oct. 20, 1684. 14/37

MACHERE, or MACHORE, David. To Jamaica. Nov. 10, 1690. (Same entry as Abraham and Isaac DECASSERIS). 15/19a

MACKERITH, William of Pickadilly (London?), bricklayer. Bound to James Finch for 4 years in Pensilvania. Age 26. April 1, 1686. 14/556

MACK GRIGGER (Probably Macgregor), Margarett, spinster of Wapping. Bound to John Pye for 4 years in Virginia. Sept. 4, 1685. 14/389

MADDIN, Mary. Daughter of James Maddin of St. Giles in the Fields (Middlesex). Bound to John Ruddes for 4 years in Virginia. Sept. 14, 1685. Witness Elizabeth Hopton. 14/400

MAJOR, Anthony. See Peter BECKFORD.

MAPLETOFT, Robert. Son of Peter Mapletoft of Stamford, Lincolne, grocer. Bound to John Meares for 4 years in Barbadoes. Sept, 14, 1685. Witness John Hill, his uncle. 14/400

MARCH, John. "Upon the affirmation of Mr. Thos. Cushy of this parish (parish not mentioned, possibly St. Lawrence Jewry?) that the said John March had constantly resided in this citie for the space of seven weeks last had a pass to New England, there to abide. July 20, 1685. 14/331

MARKHAM, Joanna. To Pensilvania. June 24, 1691. 15/40

MARRYOT, Elizabeth, spinster. Bound to John Lock for 4 years in Maryland. Age 22. Nov. 17, 1685. 14/452

MARSHALL, Elizabeth of London, spinster.   Bound to William Bartram for
6 years in Antego.   Age 16 and upwards.   Feb. 20, 1684.   14/161

MARTIN, John of Dumfrize (Dumfries), Scotland.   Bound to Hugh Horton
for 4 years in Jamaica.   Not married.   March 2, 1684.   14/167

MARTIN, John.   Same details as above except date.   March 4, 1684.
                                                                  14/169

MARTIN, John.   Son of Phillipp Martin, late of Souton (Sourton?) in Devon,
deced.   Bound to John Moorhead for 4 years in Jamaica.   May 1, 1685.
                                                                  14/229

MARTIN, John.   See Robert BLACKLOCK.

MARTIN, John of London, labourer.   Bound to William Cooke for 4 years
in Jamaica.   Oct. 31, 1684.   14/48

MARTIN, Martha.   Daughter of William Martin of St. Mary Magdalene,
Surrey.   Bound to Thomas Hunt for 4 years in Jamaica.   March 2, 1684.
                                                                  14/167

MARTIN, Thomas.   Bound to Walter Pye for 4 years in Jamaica.   Age 24.
Oct. 21, 1684.   14/39

MATHEWS, Henry of Gritworth (Greatworth), Northamptonshire, sawyer.
Bound to John Richards for 4 years in Barbadoes.   May 15, 1686.   14

MATTHEWS, Peter.   Bound to "Richards of London" for 8 years in Maryland.
July 23, 1685.   Witness Sarah Matthews of Shoe Lane (London).   14/336

MAWSON, Robert, of Gateside, Westmorland, yeoman.   Bound to John
Richards for 4 years in Barbadoes.   May 12, 1686.   14

MAYO, Lucy and her servant.   To Jamaica.   June 22, 1691.   15/39a

MEADOWES, Anne, daughter of ? of St. Sepulchers Parish in Middlesex,
shoemaker.   Bound to John Lightfoot for 5 years in Virginia.   July 9, 1684.
Witness Elizabeth Child, her sister.   13

MEALES, John.   See Peter BECKFORD.

MEERS, Isaac. To Jamaica. Nov. 10, 1690. 15/19a

MEAX, John. To Jamaica. Nov. 11, 1690 15/20a

MECHIN, William. Bound to Charles Richards for 4 years in Jamaica.
Age 20. April 19, 1686. 14/605

MIDDLETON, Mary. Bound to John Moorehead for 4 years in Barbadoes.
Age 21. April 10, 1685. 14/218

MIDGKEE, Henry. Son of John Midgkee, late of Bletchenlye (Bletchingly),
Surrey, dyer, deced. Bound to John Newyer for 4 years in Jamaica.
Nov. 7, 1684. 14/51

MIEGLEY, Elizabeth, spinster. Bound to Richard Phillipps for 5 years in
Maryland. Age 23. July 27, 1685. 14/345

MILBURNE, James. Son of Nicholas Milburne, late of Bishop Auckland,
Durham, Deced. Bound to Arthur Elliot for 4 years in Virginia. Dec. 1,
1684. 14/82

MILLER, Mary, widow. Bound to William Smith for 4 years in Pensilvania.
June 23, 1684. 13

MILLS, Sarah. Daughter of Henry Mills of Hansam (Horsham or Hailsham?)
in Sussex, deced. Bound to Joseph North for 4 years in Jamaica. Age 18.
Dec. 6, 1684. Mary Hobson witnessed that she was not married. 14/89

MILLS, Thomas. Bound to Robert Shanks for 4 years in Virginia. Aug. 27,
1684. 13

MILLS, William of London, labourer. Bound to James Williams for 4 years
in Barbadoes. Age 26. March 20, 1684. Has neither wife nor child.
14/192

MOLLONE, Charles and SHAW, Denny. Two Irishmen. Bound to John
Moorhead for 4 years in Jamaica. April 28, 1685. (Same entry as
Charles TAYLOR). 14/228

MONGOMERY, Anne. Daughter of Robert Mongomery of Newcastle (probably Upon-Tyne), waterman. Bound to Robert Burman for 5 years in
Maryland. July 15, 1684. 13

MOORE, George of St. Gyles in the Feilds, carpenter.   Bound to Charles
Richards for 4 years in Jamaica.   March 22, 1685.   14/547

MOORE, John, glass bottle maker.   Bound to Joseph Martin (agent for the
Pensilvania Society) for 4 years in Pensilvania.   March 10, 1683.   13

MOORE, Sarah.   Wife of Richard Moore, distiller in Barbadoes. Nov. 11,
1690.   15/20a

MORGAN, Margarett.   Daughter of Richard Morgan of St. Giles in the
Fields, Middlesex.   Bound to John Lightfoot for 5 years in Virginia.
July 10, 1684.   13

MORGAN, William of London, shoemaker.   Bound to Marmaduke Larkin
for 4 years in Maryland.   Aug. 6, 1685. Witness Admond Burnham.   14/357

MORGIN, Thomas.   Son of William Morgin of Bishopsgate Street, London.
Bound to James Foster for 4 years in Mount Serratt.   March 31, 1685. 14/205

MORRICE, Martha, spinster.   Bound to Francis Morrice for 4 years in
Virginia.   Age 19.   Aug. 29, 1685.   Witness the said Francis, her uncle.
                                                                            14/384

MORRIS, Eliza.   Daughter of John Morris, late of Ewell in Surry "By consent
of Anne Strange, her aunt".   Bound to Phillipp Gower for 4 years in
Jamaica.   Age 20.   March 27, 1685.   14/199

MORRIS, Julian, spinster.   Bound to Samuel Philipps for 4 years in Maryland.
Age 15.   Oct. 23, 1685.   Witness Mary Lennell, his mother, wife of
Samuel Lennell.   14/438

MORROW, Roger.   Bound to John Dix for 4 years in Maryland.   Oct. 23,
1684.   14/41

MORTIMER, Robert.   Son of William Mortimer of Uphaven (Upavon),
Wiltshire.   Bound to Thomas Green for 4 years in Jamaica.   Nov. 14,
1684.   14/59

MORTLACK, Charles.   Son of John Mortlack of Nottingham, ironmonger.
Bound to Barbarah Orgill for 4 years in Jamaica.   Dec. 19, 1683.   13

MORTON or NORTON, John.   Son of Richard Morton or Norton of Old

Bethelem, London. Bound to James Williams for 4 years in Jamaica.
Jan. 10, 1684. 14/117

MOUNFIELD, John. Son of Thomas Mounfield of Grafham (Graffham),
Sussex, maltster, deced. Bound to John Worthington for 4 years in Maryland.
Sept. 8, 1684. 14/3

MOUNTFORD, Richard of Kinlett, Shropshire, wheelwright. Bound to
Rowland Buckley for 4 years in Barbadoes. April 1, 1685. 14/206

MUNDAY, Robert. Bound to William Pegson or Pogson for 4 years (no
colony stated). Age 21. Oct. 22, 1684. 14/40

MUNDY, Bridget. Bound to Nicholas Painter for 5 years in Maryland.
Aug. 21, 1684. 13

MUNDY, Nicholas. Son of Robert Mundy of Steeple Langford, Wiltshire.
Bound to John Richards for 4 years in Jamaica. Jan. 10, 1684. 14/117

MURTON, John. Son of John Murton of Kent, deced. Bound to John
Moorhead for 4 years in Jamaica. Age 22. May 2, 1685. Witness
Thomas Pattman of St. Katherines, who had known him 4 years last.
14/232

MUSGRAVE, William. Son of Daniell Musgrave, late of Codleman
(Godalming?) in Surrey, husbandman, deced. Bound to Thomas Green for
7 years in Virginia. Nov. 8, 1684. 14/52

N

NELL, Thomas of London, labourer.   Bound to Robert Shanks for 4 years in
Jamaica.   Age 22.   Nov. 24, 1684.   14/73

NEVISTON, William.   Son of John Neviston, late of Ireland.   Bound to
Thomas Newbold for 8 years in Virginia.   July 25, 1685.   14/341

NEWARKE, William.   Son of John Newarke of London.   Bound to John
Salmon to serve in Jamaica.   (No term stated).   Age 19.   Feb. 16, 1684.
                                                                       14/157

NEWMAN, Mary.   Daughter of William Newman of Sunderidge (Sundridge),
Kent, gentleman, deced.   Bound to John Tanner for 4 years in Maryland.
Age 22.   Aug. 10, 1685.   Consent of her mother testified by Sibilla
Dunn.   14/362

NEWTON, Elizabeth.   Bound to William Boulton for 4 years in Virginia.
July 22, 1685.   Witness Ann Forger, Wapping, (London).   14/334

NEWTON, Francis.   Bound to Robert Roadds for 4 years in Jamaica.   Age 21.
May 5, 1685.   "Her father and mother living in Cock Alley in Shoreditch"
(Middlesex.)   14/238

NEWTON, Hugh.   Bound to Christopher Jefferson for 4 years 9 months in
St. Christophers.   Feb. 15, 1685.   14/523

NICCOLL, Andrew.   Bound to Archibald Arthur for 4 years in Virginia.
Age 24.   Sept. 22, 1684.   14/15

NICHOLLS, Dorothy.   Bound to Barthew Biggs for 4 years in Barbadoes.
Nov. 7, 1684.   14/51

NICCOLLS, Joseph.   Son of Thomas Niccolls, Woolledge (Woolwich), Kent.
Bound to Symon Bashford for 7 years in Virginia.   Age 12.   Oct. 10, 1685.
Witness Jane Niccolls, his mother.   14/427

NICHOLSON, George.   To New England. Nov. 15, 1690.   15/23

NOBLE, William, of Christchurch, Southwarke. Bound to Richard Heath for 4 years in Maryland. June 30, 1685. 14/306

NORRIS, John of London, porter. Bound to John Cutcher for 4 years in Jamaica. Age 26. Oct. 1, 1685. Witness his mother, Eleanor. 14/420

NORRIS, Thomas of Lester (Leicester). Bound to Thomas Nicholls for 4 years in Pensilvania or W. Jersey. Age 22. April 21, 1686. 14/608

NORTON, John. See MORTON.

NORTON, Thomas. Son of Thomas Norton, labourer. Bound to Matthew Trimm for 4 years in Virginia. Oct. 21, 1684. 14/39

NORWOOD, Mary. Daughter of Edward Norwood, tinker, deced. Bound to William Lock for 4 years in Mount Serratt. April 10, 1685. 14/217

O

OLDFIELD, John.   Bound to Abraham Wilde for 4 years in Maryland.
Aug. 21, 1684.   13

OLIVEAR, John.   Bound to Robert Shanks for 4 years in Virginia.   Oct. 14,
1684.   14/30

ORRILL, Mary.   Daughter of Richard Orrill of Hatton Garden, (London).
Bound to Joseph Bartholemew for 4 years in Jamaica.   Age 19.   March 27,
1685.   14/199

OSBORNE, Daniell.   Son of Thomas Osborne of Stow Markett, Suffolk,
hatband maker, deced.   Bound to Thomas Tench for 4 years in Maryland.
Aug. 11, 1684.   13

OSBORNE, Joseph.   Son of Joseph Osborne.   Bound to Thomas Nichols for
7 years in Pensilvania or West Jersey.   Age 15.   April 19, 1686.   Witnesses
Joseph his father and Margarett, his mother.   14/605

OUBLEY, Owen.   Son of Edward Oubley, Cobham, Surrey, coachman,
deced.   Bound to Raineford Waterhouse for 4 years in Jamaica.   Age 23.
Dec. 29, 1684.   14/108

OVERDELL, William.   Son of William Overdell of St. Ollaves, Surrey.
Bound to Richard Heath for 7 years in Maryland.   July 11, 1684.   13

OWEN, Margarett.   Daughter of Richard Owen, late of Coleman Street,
London, packer, deced.   Bound to Richard Fyfe for 5 years in Maryland.
Aug. 13, 1684.   13

P

PAINE, Hester. Daughter of Harbett Paine, Shawditch, Middlesex, deced.
Bound to Joseph Athy for 4 years in Mount Serrat. Age 23. Feb. 1, 1685.
Witness William Bradshaw   (Same entry as Elizabeth BOOTH).   14/510

PAINE, John. Son of Richard Paine of Bastable (Barnstaple), Devon.
Bound to Robert Shanks for 4 years in Jamaica. Age 23. Jan. 3, 1684.
14/112

PALLMER, William of Armitage (?), Middlesex. Bound to John Williams
for 4 years in Barbadoes. May 1, 1685. Witness Benjamin Annall of same
place.   14/229

PALMER, Mathew. Bound to Thomas Lee for 4 years in Virginia. Age 18.
Dec. 15, 1685.   14/479

PALMER, Sarah, spinster. Bound to John Dikes for 4 years in Jamaica.
Age 23.   March 9, 1684.   14/177

PARKER, Armstrong. Son of George Parker of Asleckton (Aslockton) in
Vale of Belvoyer (?), Nottingham. Bound to Anthony Guest for 7 years in
Virginia.   Oct. 9, 1685.   14/427

PARKER, Charles. Son of Charles Parker of Eckle (Eccleshall?), Stafford-
shire, mason, deced. Bound to John Moorhead for 4 years in Jamaica.
Age 26. May 1, 1685. "Lodged halfe a yeare in house of Richard and
Mary Wareing".   14/230

PARKER, Elizabeth, spinster. Bound to Emmanuel Winsor for 4 years in
America.   Aug. 21, 1684.   13

PARKER, William. Bound to John Fleming to serve in Jamaica (no term
given).   Feb. 14, 1682.   13

PARR, Thomas. Son of Thomas Parr of Aldersgate Street (London) by the
consent of Susannah Parr, his mother. Bound to Barnaby Cater for 5 years
in Barbadoes.   April 30, 1685.   14/228

PARSONS, Elizabeth.   Daughter of Richard Parsons of Gloucester (city), spinster.   Bound to Joseph Athy for 4 years in Montserrat.   Age 20.   Feb. 13, 1685.   Her father's consent affirmed by William Pott.   14/521

PARSONS, William.   To Jamaica.   Nov. 15, 1690.   15/23

PASHELLOR, Anne.   Daughter of William Pashellor of Beech Lane, lead refiner of Criplegate (London).   Bound to Alexander Rowland for 4 years in Jamaica.   Age 18.   May 19, 1686.   Witnesses her father and Anne, her mother-in-law.   14

PASSELL, Sarah.   Daughter of Jonathan Passell of Tilbury, Kent (Tilbury is in Essex).   Bound to Richard Cornwallis for 5 years in Virginia.   Oct. 9, 1684.   14/29

PATRONE, Jean Louys.   See CALIGNON, Edward.

PATTISON, Edward Junior.   See PATTISON, Edward Senior.

PATTISON, Edward Senior, with Elizabeth, his wife, Edward PATTISON Junior, Sarah PATTISON, Sarah SWETMAN, Ralph GREATOREX, Katherine GREATOREX.   To Jamaica.   Nov. 14, 1690.   15/22

PATTISON, Elizabeth.   See PATTISON, Edward.

PATTISON, Sarah.   See PATTISON, Edward.

PAWLING, Elizabeth, spinster.   Bound to John Burford for 4 years in Maryland.   Age 21.   Aug. 25, 1685.   Witness Sarah Read, Wapping.   14/379

PAYNE, John of Norfolk.   Bound to John Gibbs for 5 years in Carolina.   13 Feb. 26, 1682.

PAYTON, Joshua.   Son of John Payton of London, saylor, deced.   Bound to John Wynn for 8 years in Virginia.   Sept. 26, 1684.   14/19

PEATE, Elizabeth, spinster.   Bound to James Mathew for 7 years in Jamaica. June 16, 1684.   13

PEGSON, Katherine and Mary.   Servants to Wm. Harris.   To Barbadoes. Nov. 13, 1690.   15/21a

PEGSON, Mary.   See Katherine PEGSON.

PEIRCE, Thomas.   Son of Thomas Peirce of Kingston on Thames, plaisterer, deced.   Bound to Thomas Tench for 4 years in Maryland.   Aug. 7, 1684.

13

PEIRSON, Thomas.   Son of William Peirson of Shoe Lane, St. Brides, London, feltmaker.   Bound to Edward Tomlin for 7 years in Virginia. Dec. 8, 1685.   14/473

PENELLICK, Humphrey.   Bound to Marmaduke Larkin for 4 years in Maryland.   July 23, 1685.   Witness Chicester Young his relation, of Middle Temple, London.   14/337

PEPPER, Jane of London, widow.   Bound to William Bartram for 4 years in Antego.   Feb. 20, 1684.   Has no children.   14/161

PEPPER, Susan.   Daughter of John Pepper, marriner of Wallnut Ally, Southwark, (Surrey).   Bound to Anthony Dent for 5 years in Virginia. Aug. 20, 1685.   Witness Adrie Woodburne, her aunt.   (See Mary WOOD-BURNE).   14/374

PEREGOIS, Joseph.   "A Frenchman, being of full age".   Bound to Robert Burman for 5 years in Maryland.   July 21, 1685.   14/333

PERRY, Henry.   Son of Henry Perry of Hackney, Middlesex, butcher, deced. Bound to John Dangerfield for 5 years in Virginia.   Sept. 10, 1685. Witness, Susanna Perry, his mother.   14/393

PETTO, Abraham.   Bound to John Williams for 4 years in Virginia.   Age 21. March 12, 1684.   14/181

PHILIGOT, Philip.   Son of Odo Philigot of Paris, France, woolspinner. Bound to Rene Drignion for 4 years in Pensilvania.   May 1, 1684.   13

PHILIPPS, Edward.   To Maryland.   June 24, 1691.   15/40

PHILLIPPS, Christopher.   Son of John Phillipps in Cornwall, husbandman. Bound to John Richard for 4 years in Maryland "To serve him in Maryland after the next arrivall of the good shipp called the Virginia Factor there". Oct. 18, 1684.   14/36

PILCHER, Stephen. Son of Stephen Pilcher of Sandwich, Kent, merchant, deced. Bound to Richard Fyfe for 5 years in Maryland. Aug. 13, 1684.

13

PIPPIN, Mary. Daughter of John Pippin, Strand, Middlesex, deced. (Either a London street or the hamlet of Strand Green). Bound to John Tanner for 4 years in Maryland. Age 21. Aug. 10, 1685. Witness Mary Litherland, her aunt.

14/362

PITHIBRIDGE, Mary, widow. Bound to Joseph Bartholemew for 4 years in Jamaica. Age 22. May 7, 1685.

14/241

PITTS, Mary. Daughter of William Pitts, marriner of Greenwich, Kent. deced. Bound to Philip Gower to serve in Jamaica (no term stated). April 9, 1685.

14/216

PLUMPTON, John, of London, labourer. Bound to Thomas Green for 4 years in Jamaica. Oct. 31, 1684.

14/47

POLLARD, Jeffery. Son of William Pollard, Allhallows the Less, London, porter. Bound to Samuel Ayres for 4 years in Barbadoes. March 3, 1685. Witnesses Sarah Pollard, his mother and John Huffam, his master.

14/535

POLLARD, Joane, spinster. Bound to Abraham Wilde for 4 years in Maryland. Aug. 18. 1684.

13

POND, Mary. Daughter of Abraham Pond, Margett (Margate), Kent, Innkeeper. Bound to Richard Heath for 4 years in Maryland "with this condition that if in a week she desires to stay and not to go to Maryland, he is to discharge her, payeing 5 shillings and 6 pence charges". Age 21. July 25, 1684. (Anne Pickering and Mary Pond haveing pilfered a paire of stayes and several other things from her master and Mary Barnes haveing received part of the same goods and encouraged them, committed to Bridewell, (prison) July 24, 1684")

13

PORIS, Katherine, spinster. Bound to David Lockwood for 4 years in Jamaica. Age 24. Dec. 19, 1684.

14/101

POSTERNE, Elizabeth. Daughter of William Posterne, late of Blackfriars, London, glover, deced. Bound to Nicholas Richardson for 4 years in Jamaica. Oct. 11, 1684.

14/29

POUNSEY, William.   With consent of Alice Pounsey of Shadd Town in Southwark.   Bound to Richard Stephens for 8 years in Maryland.   July 22, 1685.   14/334

POWELL, Elizabeth of Whitechappell.   Bound to Samuel Roberts for 8 years in Maryland. Sept. 19, 1685. Witness Elizabeth Powell, her mother. (See also Joseph POWELL).   14/406

POWELL, Isaac.   Son of Oliver Powell, worsted comber, deced.   Bound to Mathew Trimm for 4 years in Jamaica.   Oct. 21, 1684.   14/39

POWELL, Joseph.   Brother of Elizabeth POWELL, q. v.   Bound to Samuel Roberts for 9 years in Virginia. Sept. 19, 1685.   14/406

POYNER, Thomas.   "Thomas POYNER and Mary TATE, late prisoners in New Prison, upon the afirmacion of Adam Turnbull, turnkey of the said prison, that they were taken up late at night and were not comitted by cot. (court?) and that there was no other charge against them and that they were not married nor apprentices, bound themselves to John Furle of Wapping, marriner, to serve in Maryland 4 years". July 21, 1685.   14/333

PRATT, Edward.   Bound to Nathaniel Redman for 5 years in Jamaica. Age 15.   April 9, 1686.   14/600

PRETTY, Anne.   Daughter of William Pretty, late of Old Windsor in Berkshire, deced.   Bound to Joseph Bartholemew for 4 years in Jamaica. Age 16.   April 14, 1685.   14/219

PRICE, Elizabeth, spinster.   Bound to Christopher Keen for 2 years in Jamaica.   Nov. 19, 1685. Witness Stephen Keen, instrument maker.
                                                                  14/454

PRICE, Thomas.   Son of Thomas Price, labourer.   Bound to Richard Smith for 9 years in Maryland.   Age 13.   Sept. 1, 1685.   14/387

PRINE, John.   Bound to Anthony Gester for 4 years in Virginia.   Age 20. Sept. 21, 1685.   Witness John Prine of Ratcliffe, his father.   14/409

PROCTER, George.   Son of William Procter of Wedgbury (Wednesbury?), Staffordshire, taylor.   Bound to Thomas Tench for 6 years in Maryland. Aug. 5, 1684.   13

PROVIST, John.   Son of John Provist, late of St. Gyles in the Fields, deced. "His mother also deced, by consent of his sister".   Bound to James Parsons for 4 years in Jamaica.   Age 18.   Dec. 5, 1684.   14/87

PROWDMAN, William.   Son of William Prowdman, late of London. Bound to William Emberley for 5 years in Barbadoes.   Dec. 15, 1684.   14/95

PRYOR, Mathew of Norfolke, Labourer.   Bound to John Gibbs for 5 years in Carolina.   March 2, 1682.   13

PULLMAN, Robert.   Bound to Thomas Nicholls for 7 years in Pensilvania or West Jersey.   Age 15.   April 20, 1686.   Witness Elizabeth Pullman, his mother, of Wapping (now London).   14/606

PURCHASE or PURCHIS, Daniell.   Son of John Purchis, late of St. Mary Odrey (Ottery St. Mary?), Devon, chandler, deced.   Bound to David Lockwood for 4 years in Jamaica.   Nov. 4, 1684.   14/49

PURTON, Jane.   Bound to Gilber Ashly for 4 years in New Providence. Oct. 22, 1683.   13

Q

QUICK, Mary.   Daughter of Catherine Taylor (q. v.) and Christopher Quick.   Bound to Mathew Tazzard for 4 years in Nevis.   Oct. 20, 1685.
                    14/435

R

RAINES, Charles of Long Acre, London, carpenter, and Mary, his wife. Bound to Charles Richards for 4 years in Jamaica. March 30, 1686. (See also William and Elizabeth RICHARDS). 14/553

RAINES, Mary. See Charles RAINES.

RAKES, Phillis. Bound to Robert Portern for 4 years in Antego. March 13, 1684. 14/183

RAMEAGE, Elizabeth, spinster. Bound to Thomas Nicholls for 6 years in Pensilvania. Age 18. April 9, 1686. Witness Susannah Rameage, her mother, widow, of the Minories (London). 14/559

RANDALL, Matthew. Bound to Abraham Wilde for 4 years in Maryland. Aug. 18, 1684. 13

RANDALL, Nicholas. Bound to John Richards for 4 years in Barbados. April 29, 1686. Witness William Attwell. 14/618

RANDALL, Thomas. Son of Thomas Randall, late of Cheshunt in the county of Hareford (Hertford), deced. Bound to Thomas Sawell for 4 years in Jamaica. Age 20 or thereabouts. May 28, 1685. Witness William Randall of Old Bethlem, shoemaker. 14/265

RAWLINGS, Richard. Bound to William Emberry for 4 years in Barbadoes. Age 23. March 10, 1684. 14/178

RAWLINS, Mary. Daughter of John Rawlins, Bednall Green (Bethnall Green), Middlesex, deced. Bound to John Rafe for 7 years in Virginia. July 30, 1685. Witnesses Christopher Sandon, Minories (London), looking glass maker and John Towers, Bednall Green, her father-in-law. 14/348

RAYMOND, Edward. Bound to Thomas Hall for 4 years in Jamaica. Age 20. Dec. 14, 1685. Witness Saintclear Raymond of Winchester Park, Southwark (Surrey), his father. 14/478

RAYNER, William.   Bound to John Clarke for 4 years in Virginia.   Age 17.
Sept. 26, 1685.   14/418

READ, Mary.   "The servant of Jane Coffill, her misstress consenting freely
to part with her".   Bound to Richard Heath for 4 years in Maryland.   July
25, 1684.   (Entry above reads: Committed to Bridewell: Mary Read, for
pilfering two chickens out of the shop of John Corfield, maister. July 22,
1684".   13

READ, William.   Son of William Read deced.   Bound to Mathew Huberd
for 7 years in Virginia.   Oct. 20, 1684.   14/38

READ, William.   Son of Michaell Read of Bullwell, Nottingham, deced.
Bound to Robert Shanks for 4 years in Jamaica.   Nov. 11, 1684.   14/56

REAMES, Thomas.   Son of Thomas Reames, late of Faversham in Kent,
farmer.   Bound to William Bonniface for 4 years in Jamaica.   Age 40.
May 19, 1685.   14/258

REEKES, Robert, of Kingston, Dorset, labourer.   Bound to David Lockwood
for 4 years in Jamaica.   Age 21.   Oct. 27, 1684.   14/45

REEPE, Samuel.   Bound to Charles Richards for 4 years in Jamaica.   Age 19.
April 17, 1686.   14/602

REYNAULT, Elizabeth.   Daughter of Henry Reynault (q. v.)   Bound to
Marmaduke Larkin for 6 years in Jamaica.   Aug. 3, 1685.   (See note
under ANBIER).   14/353

REYNAULT, Elizabeth.   Wife of Henry REYNAULT (q. v.)   Also, see note
under ANBIER.   14/353

REYNAULT, Francois of London, labourer.   Bound to Marmaduke Larkin
for 4 years in Jamaica.   "By Henry REYNAULT, his father's consent".
Aug. 3, 1685.   (See REYNAULT, Henry and also ANBIER)   14/353

REYNAULT, Henry of London, labourer, and Elizabeth his wife.   A French
man and woman bound to Marmaduke Larkin for 4 years in Jamaica.
Aug. 3, 1685.   (Also Francois, his son and Elizabeth and Marie, his
daughters).   14/353

REYNAULT, Marie, daughter of Henry REYNAULT (q. v.).   Bound to

Marmaduke Larkin for 7 years in Jamaica.   Aug. 3, 1685.   (See note under ANBIER).   14/353

REYNOLDS, Elizabeth.   Daughter of John Reynolds, late of Cornwall (perhaps meant for Cornwood?) in Devonshire.   Bound to Barnaby Cater for 4 years in Barbadoes.   April 30, 1685.   14/229

REYNOLDS, Thomas.   "By consent of Ann Reynolds, his mother".   Bound to John Yanows for 9 years in Virginia.   Sept. 16, 1684.   14/9

RICHARDS, William and Elizabeth, his wife.   Brother-in-law to Charles Raines (q. v.), Elizabeth Richards being Charles Raines's sister.   Raines, his wife and William and Elizabeth Richards all under one entry.   Bound to Charles Richards for 4 years in Jamaica.   March 30, 1686.   14/553

RICHARDSON, Martha.   Daughter of William Richardson, late of York, pewterer, deced.   Bound to Robert Shanks for 4 years in Virginia.   Sept. 30, 1684.   (Under same entry as Mary HAYKINS).   14/22

RIDGELL, William.   Bound to Robert Shanks for 4 years in Jamaica. Oct. 27, 1684.   14/46

RINE, John of Craford (Crayford), Kent.   Bound to John Gibbs for 5 years in Barbadoes.   Age 18.   Jan. 20, 1684.   14/129

RISE, Mary.   Daughter of Thomas Rise, late of Shoreditch, shoemaker, deced.   Bound to Christopher Eyre for 4 years in Jamaica.   May 6, 1685.
                                                                        14/238

RITHER, James, "having no friends".   Bound to John Pheasant for 7 years in Virginia.   Age 13.   Nov. 23, 1685.   14/459

ROBERTS, Francis,   bricklayer.   Son of William Roberts of Bristol, taylor. Bound to James Williams for 4 years in Jamaica.   Age 30.   May 1, 1685.
                                                                        14/231

ROBERTS, William.   Pass to Jamaica.   Nov. 1, 1692.   Ref. Court Book for 1692-5.

ROBERTS, William.   Son of William Roberts, St. Butts (Botolph), Aldersgate, deced.   Bound to William Frisby for 12 years in Maryland.   Aug. 1, 1684.   13

ROBINSON, Daniell. Bound to John Richards for 7 years in Barbadoes.
Age 17. April 27, 1686. Witnesses George Kewland, his father-in-law
and Deborah, his mother. 14/616

ROBINSON, Rebeccah. Bound to John Robinson for 4 years in Jamaica.
Age 19. May 1, 1686. Witness Mary Trevailer. (Same entry as Mary
HUTTON and Joane BROWNE). 14/621

ROBINSON, Samuel. Bound to John Williams for 4 years in Virginia.
Age 21. March 12, 1684. 14/182

ROGER, Allian of London, labourer. Bound to Robert Shanks for 4 years in
Jamaica. Age 35. Nov. 28, 1684. (See also Caleb ROGER, his son.)
14/77

ROGER, Caleb. Son of Allian ROGER (q.v.). Bound to Robert Shanks for
4 years in Jamaica. Age 15. Nov. 28, 1684. 14/77

ROGERS, John. Bound to John Gandy for 6 years in Maryland. Nov. 14,
1685. Witness Mary Parker, his mother. 14/450

ROGERS, Thomas. Son of Evan Rogers of Aucestry (Oswestry?), Shropshire,
labourer, deced. Bound to Elizabeth Weeks for 6 years in Virginia.
Nov. 7, 1685. 14/443

ROGERS, William of Newn(h)am, Northamptonshire, blacksmith. Bound
to John Richards for 4 years in Barbadoes. Nov. 10, 1684. 14/55

ROSE, William, clerk. To Jamaica. Nov. 10, 1690. 15/19a

ROSSE, John. Son of Humphrey Rosse, late of Cambridge, bricklayer,
deced. Bound to Samuell Phipps for 4 years in Virginia. Oct. 7, 1684.
14/27

ROULSTON, Sarah. Bound to Arthur Easdell for 4 years in Virginia.
Nov. 7, 1684. 14/51

ROWLAND, William. Son of John Rowland, late of Shoreditch, brewers
clarke, deced. Bound to Samuell Woodfield for 5 years in Virginia. Age
18. July 18, 1685. Witness Rebeccah Rowland, his mother 14/330

ROWLEY, John, of Long Sutton, Lincolnshire, husbandman. Bound to

James Williams for 4 years in Barbadoes.   Age 22.   May 11, 1686.   14

ROWTON, Samuel.   Bound to Thomas Nixon for 5 years in Virginia.
Age 13.   March 15, 1685.   Witness Henry Arthur, his father-in-law. 14/544

ROYSTON, John.   Son of Robert Royston.   Bound to Robert Burman for 5
years in Maryland.   July 21, 1685.   14/333

RUSS, James.   Son of John Russ of Bemcroft Hill in the Parish of Brimhill
(Bremhill), Wiltshire.   Bound to Robert Shanks for 4 years in Jamaica.
Age 22 or thereabouts.   Dec. 2, 1684.   14/85

RUSSELL, Laurence.   A French boy.   Bound to John Boullay for 7 years in
Maryland.   Age 14.   Sept. 5, 1685.   Witness Abraham Michael, his
cozen, a Frenchman of Dorsett Street, Spittlefields (London).   14/391

RUSSELL, Thomas of Wanstead, Essex, husbandman.   Bound to Rowland
Buckley for 4 years in Barbadoes.   Age 23.   A single man.   March 27,
1685.   14/199

RUST, Daniel of Norwich.   Bound to Thomas Tench for 4 years in Maryland.   July 28, 1684.   13

RUST, John.   Son of Thomas Rust of Ellsham (Aylsham), Norfolk.   Bound
to Richard Adams for 4 years in Jamaica.   Nov. 10, 1684.   14/56

S

SAINT, James. Son of James Saint of Flashbrook, Staffordshire, deced.
Bound to Joseph Pyle for 4 years in Maryland.   July 19, 1684.   13

SAMPSON, Francis.   Bound to William Winter for 4 years in Virginia.
Age 20.   Dec. 14, 1685.   14/479

SAVAGE, John. Son of Abraham Savage, late of Canterbury, weaver, deced.
Bound to Thomas Taylor for 5 years in Virginia.   Oct. 7, 1684.   (Brother
of Thomas SAVAGE, q.v.)   14/27

SAVAGE, Thomas.   Son of Abraham Savage, late of Canterbury, weaver,
deced.   Bound to Thomas Taylor for 6 years in Virginia.   Oct. 7, 1684.
(Brother of John, above; different term of service).   14/27

SAVAGE, William.   Son of Francis Savage of Blankney, (Lincolnshire).
blacksmith, deced.   Bound to David Lockwood for 4 years in Jamaica.
Nov. 7, 1684..   14/51

SAVERY, Mary, spinster.   Bound to Abraham Wilde for 4 years in Maryland.
Aug. 18, 1684.   13

SAY, Isacaell.   Bound to Thomas Walsh for 5 years in Virginia.   Nov. 10,
1683.   13

SCALE, Joseph.   Son of William Scale of Hempstead (Hemel Hempstead),
Hertfordshire, Labourer.   Bound to Thomas Tenche for 4 years in Maryland.
Aug. 13, 1684.   13

SCARBOROUGH, William of Northampton, haberdasher.   Bound to
Christopher Squire for 4 years in Jamaica.   Oct. 15, 1684.   14/31

SCHOALE, John.   Son of Ralph Schoale of Wakefield, Yorkshire, deced.
Bound to George Elwes for 4 years in "Maryland in Virginia".   Age 25.
Sept. 7, 1685.   14/392

SCOFELL, Bridget, spinster.   Bound to Margaret Skinner for 4 years in

Jamaica.　Age 23.　Oct. 22, 1685.　Witness Elizabeth Scoffell (Relationship not stated).　　　　14/437

SCORFFEILD, Francis.　Son of James Scorfield of Eml(e)y, Yorkshire, husbandman, deced.　Bound to John Bayne for 4 years in Maryland.　Age 21.　Dec. 5, 1685.　　　　14/469

SCOTT, Joseph.　Son of Caleb Scott of London, cooper, deced.　Bound to John Hill for 5 years in Barbadoes.　Oct. 2, 1684.　　　　14/23

SEABIN, Edward.　Son of John Seabin of Wardington, Oxfordshire.　Bound to Philip Gowre for 4 years in Jamaica.　March 6, 1684.　　　　14/170

SEARCH, Elizabeth.　Daughter of Joseph Search, deced.　Bound to John Heslewood for 5 years in Virginia.　July 22, 1684.　　　　13

SEECELL, Joshua, goldsmith.　Bound to Marmaduke Larkin for 4 years in Maryland.　July 23, 1685.　　　　14/338

SELLBY, William.　Son of Robert Sellby of Peterborough in Northamptonshire.　Bound to John Moorhead for 5 years in Jamaica.　April 30, 1685.　Witness Ambrose Cox of Rosemary Lane, London.　(Perhaps Ambrose Cock who was agent for so many indentured servants later.　See Kaminkow's Emigrants, 1718-1759).　　　　14/229

SELWOOD, Elizabeth, spinster.　Bound to Margaret Skinner for 4 years in Jamaica.　Oct. 22, 1685.　Witness Anne Ratcliffe, her cozen.　　　　14/437

SEWELL, John.　Bound to Abraham Wilde for 7 years in Maryland.　Discharged out of Bridewell (prison).　Aug. 19, 1684.　　　　13

SHAW, Denny.　See MOLLONE, Charles.

SHEENE or SHEEN, John.　Son of John Sheen of Lewsam (Lewisham), Kent (now London), watchmaker, deced.　Bound to Robert Shanks for 4 years in Jamaica.　Nov. 4, 1684.　　　　14/49

SHELLEY, Joseph.　Bound to John Moorhead for 4 years in Barbadoes.　Age 21.　April 10, 1685.　　　　14/217

SHEPPARD, Anne, spinster.　Bound to Alice Bare for 4 years in Nevis.　Age 22.　Nov. 19, 1685.　Witness Suzanna Clifford, q. v.　　　　14/454

SHERBORNE, Justinian.   To New England.   Nov. 11, 1690.   15/20

SHIMPSON, Martha.   Daughter of Richard Shimpson of Norwich, butcher, deced.   Bound to Roger Newman for 5 years in Virginia.   Age 18.   Aug. 11, 1685.   14/364

SHIPWASH, Ambrose of Oxfordshire.   Bound to Philip Clarke for 7 years in Maryland.   July 25, 1684.   13

SHRIMPTON or SCRIMPTON, Epaphrai?.   See John BELL.

SIGSWORTH, Katherine, spinster.   Daughter of Thomas Sigsworth.   Bound to Matthew Trim for 4 years in Virginia.   Nov. 10, 1684.   14/56

SIMONDS, Anne, WILLIAMS, Elizabeth, EDWARDS, Jane, GURNEY, Lott. 4 servants of Richard Veysey.   Pass to Jamaica.   Nov. 13, 1690.   (See Richard VEYSEY).   15/22

SIMONS, Katherine.   Daughter of Thomas Simons of Mitcham in Surrey, deced.   Bound to John Pelly for 4 years in Barbadoes.   April 4, 1685. 14/211

SIMPKIN, John.   Son of John Simpkin of Shadwell (now London), mariner. Bound to Robert Cox for 9 years in Virginia.   Oct. 16, 1684.   14/33

SIMPSON, Abigall.   Daughter of David Simpson of Holborn (London), deced. "With the consent of Sarah Gawes of Crosslane. . St. Giles in the Fields (Middlesex), her mother".   Bound to Thomas Montagu for 4 years in Jamaica.   April 28, 1685.   14/227

SIMPSON, Elizabeth of London, spinster.   Bound to Nicholas Dove for 4 years in Jamaica.   Nov. 26, 1685.   14/460

SIMPSON, Frances of the City of Westminster, spinster.   Bound to John Triggs for 4 years in Virginia.   Nov. 26, 1684.   14/74

SIMPSON, John of London, labourer.   Bound to John Triggs for 4 years in Virginia.   Age 30 and upwards.   Nov. 26, 1684.   14/74

SIMS, Henry.   Son of Henry Sims of Somersetshire.   Bound to Robert Shanks for 6 years in Jamaica.   Oct. 16, 1684.   14/33

SKARFE, Christian. Daughter of John Skarfe of Hindwell near Whitby, Yorkshire. Bound to Silvester Wooton for 4 years in Maryland. Age 19. Aug. 17, 1685. Witness Mary Skarfe, her sister. 14/370

SKELTON, Katherine. Bound to Christopher Jefferson for 5 years in St. Christophers Feb. 20, 1685. 14/526

SLAUGHTER, John, chirurgeon. To Port Royall, Jamaica. Nov. 11, 1690. 15/20

SLEATH, William of Grimston, Leicestershire. Bound to William Martin for 4 years in Jamaica. Dec. 9, 1684. (Same entry as VYE). 14/94

SMART, Sarah. Bound to Barnaby Cater for 4 years in Barbadoes. April 28, 1685. 14/227

SMEATON, Marmaduke. Son of John Smeeton of Theeveing Lane, Bow Street, Westminster, cordwainer. Bound to Anthony Gester for 5 years in Virginia. Oct. 17, 1685. 14/433

SMEWREY, Cornelius of Berwick Upon Tweed, weaver. Bound to John Richards for 4 years in Barbadoes. Age 24. May 15, 1686. 14

SMITH, Anne, spinster. Bound to Thomas Hale for 4 years in Jamaica. Age 24. Dec. 17, 1685. Witness her brother Samuell Smith. 14/480

SMITH, Deborah. Daughter of Edward Smith of Cambridge, deced. Bound to William Flood for 4 years in Jamaica. Sept. 16, 1685. Witness Henry Moss, victualler of Royall Exchange, London, her uncle. 14/403

SMITH, Elizabeth. Daughter of James Whittle, late of Chesterfield, deced. (No county. Could be Derbyshire or Stafforshire). Bound to Richard Cornwallis for 5 years in Virginia. Oct. 9, 1684. 14/28

SMITH, Ellenor. Daughter of William Smith, gardner, deced. Bound to William Lock for 4 years in Mount Serratt. April 10, 1685. 14/217

SMITH, Hannah, spinster. Bound to John Paine for 4 years in Maryland. Sept. 28, 1685. 14/420

SMITH, John. Son of John Smith, citizen and taylor of London. Bound to Phillipp Clarke for 7 years in Maryland. Aug. 11, 1684. 13

SMITH, John. Son of Thomas Smith, late of St. Gyles in the Fields, brewers servant, deced. Bound to Edward Brooke for 7 years in Maryland. Age 14. Oct. 6, 1685. Witness Sarah Smith, his mother. 14/425

SMITH, Peter. Son of William Smith, bricklayer of London. Bound to Henry Low for 4 years in Maryland. Age 11. Nov. 28, 1684. 14/77

SMITH, Phillis. Daughter of Edward Smith, late of London. Bound to Robert Shanks for 4 years in Jamaica. Sept. 29, 1684. 14/22

SMITH, Richard. Son of George Smith, late of Cockermouth, Cumberland. Bound to John Rose for 4 years in Jamaica. Dec. 31, 1684. 14/111

SMITH, Richard. Bound to Thomas Broomer for 8 years in Virginia. Age 14. Aug. 27, 1685. Witness Anne Smith, his mother. 14/382

SMITH, Richmond. Son of John Smith of Leather Land (Lane?), Middlesex, clothdrawer. Bound to Elizabeth Norris for 4 years in Maryland. Aug. 27, 1685. 14/382

SMITH, Thomas. Bound to Philip Gower for 4 years in Barbadoes. Age 23. April 10, 1685. 14/217

SMITH, William. Son of William Smith of Scotland, deced. Bound to Richard Heath for 4 years in Maryland. July 29, 1684. 13

SMITH, William, of Longstalke (Longstock), Hampshire, vintner. Bound to John Gibbs for 5 years in Carolina. Feb. 20, 1682. 13

SMITHSON, Benjamin. Bound to Thomas Hall for 4 years in Jamaica. Age 24. Dec. 14, 1685. Witness Joshua Smith, clothworker of London Wall. 14/478

SOMERSETT, William. Son of John Somersett. "Lateley liveing in Whitechappell (London), not knowing where to find his father..." Bound to John Seaman for 9 years in Virginia. July 19, 1684. 13

SOUX, Augustine. See Edward CALIGNON.

SPEED, Hester, widow. "Her husband was slaine in the rebellion in the West." Bound to Robert Lurtinge for 5 years in Virginia. Sept. 16, 1685. Witness Mary Atkinson. 14/402

SPENCE, Richard, of Richmond, Surrey. Bound to Thomas Goddard for 4 years in Jamaica. Age 24. Oct. 16, 1685. 14/432

SPINNEDGE, Joseph, gentleman. Bound to John Viccars for 3 years in St. Christophers. Age 24. April 14, 1685. Neither wife nor children. 14/219

STACY, John. Bound to Roger Edwards for 4 years in Jamaica. Age 26. March 10, 1684. 14/179

STANDISH, Samuel. Bound to Charles Richards for 4 years in Jamaica. Age 24. April 5, 1686. 14/558

STANNICOT or STAMMINOT, Ann, spinster. Bound to John Dix for 4 years in Maryland. Age 22. Oct. 23, 1684. 14/41

STANTON, John. Bound to Robert Shanks for 4 years in Maryland. Age 26. Oct. 20, 1684. 14/37

STANTON, Robert. Son of Lawrence Stanton of St. Katherines Tower, tubman, deced. Bound to Elizabeth Wicks for 8 years in Virginia. Age 16. Witness Elizabeth Ruth, his mother. Nov. 2, 1685. 14/441

STARLING, William. Son of William Starling, late of St. John Street, Middlesex, porter, deced. Bound to Arnest Kackerbart for 7 years in Virginia. July 30, 1685. 14/348

STEELE, Isaac of London, taylor. Bound to Joseph Pendlebury for 4 years in Barbadoes. Feb. 11, 1685. 14/520

STEELE, Isaac of Nantwich, County Chester, clockmaker. Bound to Henry Hartwell for 5 years in Virginia. Age 21. Oct. 16, 1683. 13

STEPHENS, Benjamin. Bound to Richard Smith for 9 years in Maryland. Age 14. Aug. 28, 1685. Witness Abigail Stephens, widow, of Newmarket in Clare Street (London?) 14/383

STEPHENS, Henry. Bound to John Lightfoot for 12 years in Virginia. June 23, 1684. Witness Rebecca, his mother. 13

STEPHENS, John and his wife (Unnamed). To Maryland. June 24, 1691. 15/40

STEVENSON, John.   Bound to John Elliot for 4 years in Jamaica.   Age 26.
Nov. 22, 1684.   14/72

STEWART, James.   Bound to John Shaw for 4 years in Jamaica.   Age 21.
March 10, 1684.   14/179

STIFFE, Jonathan.   Brother in law to John Godfrey (q. v.).   Nov. 10, 1690
To Jamaica.   15/19a

STOREY, James.   Bound to John Richards for 4 years in Maryland.   Age 22.
Oct. 22, 1684.   14/40

STRANGE, William.   Bound to William Martin for 4 years in Barbadoes.
Age 22.   Dec. 16, 1684.   14/96

SUTOR, Jane.   Daughter of William Sutor of Blackfryers (London), deced.
Bound to Barbarah Hopps for 4 years in Jamaica.   Age 21.   May 2, 1685.
By consent of Jane Rosse of Westminster, her mother.   14/232

SWETMAN, Sarah.   See Edward PATTISON.

SWETTNAM, Frances.   Daughter of Thomas Swettnam of St. Andrews,
Holborne (London), deced.   Bound to Barnaby Cater for 4 years in Barbadoes.
Age 20.   April 30, 1685.   Consent of father in law Thomas Davies.   14/229

SYMMONS, Jonathan of London, Merchant taylor.   Bound to Thomas
Plowden for 4 years in Maryland.   July 19, 1684.   13

T

TANSLY, Thomas.   Bound to Gilbert Ashley for 4 years in New Providence.
Age 24.   Oct. 22, 1683.   13

TATE, Mary.   See Thomas POYNER.

TATTNELL, Thomas, taylor.   Bound to Philip Clarke for 4 years in
Maryland.   Aug. 19, 1684.   13

TAYLOR, Catherine.   Widow of Christopher Quick, deced.   (See Mary
Quick).   Bound to Mathew Tazzard for 4 years in Nevis.   Oct. 20, 1685.
                                                                           14/435

TAYLOR, Charles.   Son of Isaac Taylor of Redbrooke in Gloucestershire.
Bound to John Moorhead for 4 years in Jamaica.   April 28, 1685.   (Under
same entry as SHAW and MOLLONE, two Irishmen).   14/228

TAYLOR, John.   Son of Richard Taylor of Holsome Rogas (Holcombe Rogus)
Devonshire, yeoman.   Bound to Myles Staples for 4 years in Maryland.
Age 22.   Aug. 14, 1685.   14/369

TAYLOR, Mary.   Daughter of John Taylor of Newinnyard (New Inn Yard),
Shawditch (Middlesex).   Bound to John Parricke for 5 years in Maryland.
Age 19.   Aug. 18, 1685.   Witness John and Anne Taylor, her parents.
                                                                           14/372

TAYLOR, Thomas.   Son of Thomas Taylor.   Bound to William Bradley for
5 years in Jamaica.   Oct. 27, 1684.   14/46

TAYLOR, William.   Son of Richard Taylor of St. Clements Deanes (St.
Clement Danes), Middlesex, taylor.   Bound to James Hobbart for 6 years
in Jamaica.   Age 16.   Feb. 23, 1685.   14/529

THOMAS, Richard, shoemaker.   Son of Richard Thomas of the City of
Bristow (Bristol) "with consent of James Thomas, his unckle".   Bound to
Joseph Bartholemew for 4 years in Jamaica.   Age 17.   March 27, 1685.
                                                                           14/198

THOMPLINSON, John.   Son of Mathew Thomplinson of Brayfeild (Bram-
field), Hertfordshire, butcher.   Bound to Thomas Tench for 5 years in
Maryland.   July 28, 1684.   13

THOMPSON, Elizabeth, spinster.   Bound to Thomas Niccols for 4 years in
Barbadoes.   Age 25.   Jan. 14, 1685.   14/496

THOMPSON, Joseph.   Father and mother both dead.   Bound to Simon
Rogers for 7 years in Pensilvania.   Age 16.   April 9, 1686.   Witness
Richard Mercer, soldier.   14/559

THOMPSON, Rachell.   Bound to Daniel Howard for 4 years in Carolina.
April 22, 1684.   13

THORNE, Sarah.   Daughter of George Thorne of St. Martins, London.
Bound to William Wilson for 4 years in Jamaica.   Nov. 14, 1684.   14/59

THUNDER, Jane.   Bound to Bartholomew Sprint for 4 years in New York.
Age 18.   June 11, 1686.   14

THWAITES, Robert.   Son of Robert Thwaites, deced.   Bound to Richard
Smith for 7 years in Maryland.   July 27, 1685.   Witness Thomas Gregory.
                                                                         14/343

TIDWELL, Mary, spinster.   Bound to Abraham Wilde for 4 years in Maryland.
Aug. 18, 1684.   13

TOMES, John.   Son of John Tomes of Christchurch, Southwarke (Surrey),
Soldjer.   Bound to Nathaniel Bryer for 7 years in Pensilvania.   March 30,
1686.   14/553

TOMLIN, Robert.   Son of John Tomlin, Southwark (Surrey), hatter, deced.
Bound to John Baxter for 7 years in Maryland.   Sept. 3, 1685.   Witness
Elizabeth Oakes, his mother.   14/389

TOPPER, George.   Son of Christopher Topper of Berry (Bury), Sussex,
yeoman, deced.   Bound to John Taylor for 4 years in Virginia.   Sept. 6,
1685.   Witness Thomas Topper, his brother.   14/425

TOWSEY, Elizabeth.   Daughter of George Towsey of St. Annes Lane,
Westminster.   Bound to Phillipp Gower for 4 years in Jamaica.   Age 15.
March 25, 1685.   14/196

TREBATT or TRIBBET, William of Cra(y)ford, Kent.   Bound to John Gibbs for 5 years in Barbadoes.   Age 22.   Jan. 20, 1684.   14/129

TREWLOVE, William.   Son of William Trewlove, late of Priest (Prees), Shropshire, silver wire drawer, deced.   Bound to Charles Richards for 4 years in Jamaica.   May 22, 1685.   14/547

TRINITYE or TRINITIE,   James.   "With the consent of the churchwardens of Trinitye, London".   (A foundling?)   Bound to Jonathan Martin for 7 years in Barbadoes.   March 2, 1685.   14/534

TUCKER, Maurice of Ludgvan, Cornwall, labourer.   Bound to Mathew Trim for 4 years in Virginia.   Age 36.   Oct. 27, 1684.   14/45

TULLIS, Thomas.   Bound to Robert Gray for 5 years in Barbadoes.   Aug. 19, 1684.   13

TURNER, Hester.   Daughter of Thomas Turner of Plimouth, Devonshire, saylor, deced.   Bound to James Parsons for 4 years in Jamaica.   Jan. 20, 1684.   14/129

TURNER, James.   Bound to William Pegson for 3 years in St. Christophers, Age 23.   Oct. 25, 1684.   14/44

TURNER, John.   Son of John Turner of Gravesend, doctor of phisicke, deced. Bound to John Underlay for 4 years in Nevis.   Oct. 5, 1685.   Witness Martha Cull, widow, his mother.   14/423

TURNER, Samuel.   Son of Henry Turner, late of Apson (?) near Exeter, turner, deced.   Bound to Robert Shanks for 4 years in Jamaica.   Oct. 7, 1684.   14/28

TURTON, Francis.   Bound to Nicholas Moor for 4 years in Philadelphia. May 19, 1684.   13

TWIGGS, Allan.   Bound to Thomas Saywell for 4 years in Barbadoes. Age 30.   April 7, 1685.   14/214

TWYCROSSE, John of Wanstead, Essex, a single man.   Bound to Rowland Buckley for 4 years in Barbadoes "to serve him as his head groome or other businesse".   Age 23.   March 27, 1685.   (See Thomas RUSSELL).   14/199

U

UDALL, Patrick.   Bound to Daniell Hill for 5 years in Maryland.   Sept. 25, 1685.   Witness Mr. Knightly of Hackney.   14/417

UNDERWOOD, John.   Son of George Underwood, late of St. Giles in the Fields (Middlesex), victualler, deced.   Bound to Edward Brooke for 5 years in Maryland.   Age 15 and upwards.   Aug. 4, 1685.   Consent of Anne Wetheridge, his mother, living at the Barbers Pole, Almshouses, near church of St. Giles in the Fields.   14/353

UPFEILD, Ruth, spinster.   Bound to Christopher Robinson for 4 years in Virginia.   Aug. 21, 1684.   13

V

VALLIANT, John.   Bound to Samuel Phillips for 4 years in Maryland.
Oct. 15, 1685.   Witnesses Mary Devallock, his mother, living near the
Elephant and Castle in Pickadilly and of Kenny Valiant, his brother.
14/432

VANGOODINGHOUSE, John.   Bound to Elizabeth Norris for 4 years in
Maryland.   Aug. 28, 1685.   Witnesses John Hayley, his master and
Samuel Goodinghouse, his nearest relation.   14/384

VAN RIKE, Adam.   Son of John Jacobson, late of Stockholm in the Kingdom
of Sweedland, deced.   Bound to Thomas Tooly for 4 years in Jamaica.
"The said Adam being recommended to the said Tooly by his father-in-law
and his own mother now liveing in Stockholm to be bound to serve in some
of the plantations and Mr. Gilbert Heathcote, merchant, declareing to his
lordship that he beleived it to be hime".   Sept. 1, 1685.   14/387

VAUGHAUN, Thomas.   Son of John Vaughaun, late of Deptford, Kent,
farmer, deced.   Bound to John Cooper for 4 years in Barbadoes.   Aug. 1,
1685.   Witness Thomas Cooper, Southwark.   14/352

VEYSEY, Richard.   With his two servants Thomas BUTCHER and Michael
HUGGINS.   To Jamaica.   Nov. 11, 1690.   (See Anne SIMONDS)   15/20

VIELLET, Pierre of London, labourer.   Bound to Marmaduke Larkin for 4
years in Jamaica.   Aug. 3, 1685.   14/353

VIGOUREUX, Isaac, of Rochell, France.   Bound to Daniel Duthaes for 4
years in Pensilvania.   July 31, 1684.   13

VINCENT, Elizabeth, widow.   Bound to Robert Morris for 4 years in Barbadoes. Age 40. Aug. 16, 1685. Robert Musgrove of London knew her
for 3 years.   14/370

VYE, Thomas of Grimston, Leicestershire.   Bound to William Martin for
4 years in Jamaica.   Dec. 9, 1684.   (Same entry as SLEATH).   14/94

W

WAKE, John.   To Jamaica.   Nov. 10, 1690   15/19a

WAKELY, Thomas.   See Elizabeth HUMES

WALES, Margaret.   Daughter of Alexander Wales of Brightshire (Brechin?),
Angus, Scotland.   Bound to Richard Fyfe for 4 years in Maryland.
Aug. 6, 1684.   13

WALKER, Thomas.   Pass to Barbadoes.   Feb. 6, 1690.   15/28

WALL, Anne, of City of Hereford, dyer.   Bound to John Whittamore for
5 years (no place given).   Jan. 19, 1682.   13

WALTON, George, of Coxshatt (Cockshutt) in Shropshire.   Bound to George
Pye for 4 years in Jamaica.   Age 23.   Jan. 8, 1684.   14/115

WARNER, Elizabeth, spinster.   Bound to John Burford for 5 years in Maryland.   Age 21.   Aug. 25, 1685.   14/379

WARREN, Nevill.   Bound to John Dikes for 4 years in Barbadoes.   Age 23.
April 6, 1685.   14/213

WARREN, William.   Bound to Thomas Dann for 4 years in Nevis.   Age 44.
Dec. 20, 1684.   14/103

WARRINGTON, Edward.   Bound to John Pearce for 4 years in Barbadoes.
Age 16.   March 10, 1685.   Witness Francis Warrington, his father, shoemaker of Whitefryers (London).   (See below also).   14/542

WARRINGTON, Edward.   Bound to Charles Richards for 5 years in Jamaica.
Age 16.   April 8, 1686.   Witness his father, Francis Warrington,
Whitefryers, shoemaker.   (See above).   14/558

WARTON, Susanna of St. Sepulchers, London, widow.   Bound to Thomas
Nicholls for 5 years in Pensilvania.   March 31, 1686.   14/554

WATERFEILD, Mary.   See Robert WATERFEILD.

WATERFEILD, Robert and Mary his wife of St. James in the Fields, carpenter.
Bound to Charles Richards for 4 years in Jamaica.   March 22, 1685.   14/547

WATERS, Elizabeth, spinster.   Bound to Robert Thorne for 4 years in Virginia.
Age 27.   Witness Mr. Cose of Ratcliffe (London).   June 30, 1685.   14/305

WATSON, John of London, labourer.   Bound to Robert Shanks for 4 years
in Jamaica.   Age 26.   Nov. 24, 1684.   14/73

WATTS, Thomas of London, marriner.   Bound to Thomas Hunt for 4 years
in Jamaica.   Age 29.   March 20, 1684.   14/192

WATTS, Thomas.   Bound to Robert Forbes for 4 years in Jamaica.   Age 23.
April 10, 1685.   14/217

WAYTE, Anne.   To Barbadoes.   Nov. 12, 1690.   15/20a

WAYTE, John Junior.   Son of John Wayte senior.   To Jamaica.   Nov. 10,
1690.   15/19a

WEBB, Frances of Southwarke, spinster.   Bound to William Cooke for 4
years in Jamaica.   Age 25.   Nov. 27, 1684.   14/76

WELCH, James of Cra(y)ford, Kent.   Bound to John Gibbs for 3 years in
Barbadoes.   Age 28.   Jan. 20, 1684.   14/129

WELLS, Peter of Little Waltham, Essex.   By consent of his brothers, John
Wells of St. George's, Southwark and James Wells of St. Katherines,
London.   Bound to Micajah Perry for 4 years in Virginia.   March 4, 1684.
                                                                       14/169

WELLS, Stephen.   Son of John Wells of Suffolke, blacksmith.   Bound to
Robert Burman for 5 years in Maryland.   July 21, 1685.   Witness, his uncle,
John Lucas of Ivy Lane, London.   14/332

WESTON, Philadelphia.   "Philadelphia Weston came before his Lordship and
declared herselfe willing to go to Virginia as a servant to the Lady Berkley
and her friends now present declared their consent also to her so dowing, of
which his Lordship granted them a certificate..."   Sept. 30, 1685.   14/420

WETTON, William of London, labourer.   Bound to Robert Shanks for 4 years in Jamaica.   Oct. 31, 1684.   14/47

WHALEY of WALEY, Richard.   Son of Richard Whaley, late of Great Marlow, Buckinghamshire, deced.   Bound to David Browne for 4 years in Virginia.   Oct. 6, 1684.   14/26

WHEATLEY, Henry.   See Joseph WRIGHT.   Same entry, same details.
                                                                14/557

WHEATLY, Penelope, spinster.   Bound to Robert Eldridge for 4 years in Virginia.   Age 21.   Jan. 14, 1685.   14/496

WHITBY, Henry.   Son of Thomas Whitby of London, porter.   Bound to Richard Bull for 4 years in Maryland.   Sept. 25, 1684.   (See below).   14/18

WHITBY or WHITTBY, Henry.   Son of Thomas Whitby of London, porter. Bound to William Hill for 4 years in Maryland.   Oct. 15, 1684.   (See above).
                                                                14/31

WHITE, Ann.   Daughter of John White, late of Lambeth in Surry, deced. Bound to Samuell Bradway for 4 years in Jamaica.   Age 23.   May 26, 1685. Witness Margaret Bidle of Brick Lane in White Chapple, her aunt.   14/264

WHITE, Miles.   Bound to Robert Shanks for 4 years in Jamaica.   Age 30. Nov. 22, 1684.   14/72

WHITE, Nicholas.   Son of John White of London, hostler.   Bound to William Holliday for 10 years in Maryland.   Aug. 24, 1685.   14/378

WHITE, Walter.   Son of Edward White of Corke in Ireland.   Bound to Robert Shanks for 4 years in Jamaica.   Nov. 12, 1684.   14/57

WHITEFIELD, Barbarah, widow.   Daughter of Edward Scholler, late of Isles of Arkney in Stonesey (Stonsay in Orkney?) in the Kingdome of Scotland, husbandman, deced.   Bound to Ernesto Keckerbart for 4 years in Virginia. Age 26.   Aug. 12, 1685.   14/365

WHITEHEAD, Jonathan.   Son of Nimian Whitehead of Southwark, barber. Bound to William Saracold for 6 years in Virginia.   Sept. 14, 1685. Witness Jane, his mother-in-law.   14/400

WHITEHEAD, William.   Son of Samuel Whitehead of Southwark.   Bound to Richard Heath for 8 years in Maryland.   Age 13.   July 6, 1685. Witnesses Samuel Whitehead, his brother and Gabriel Wilkinson.   14/317

WHITEING, John.   "John Whiteing, blacksmith, aged 20 years and upwards, haveing bin a prisoner in the Wood Street compter above ten weeks and noe freinds to assist him was bound apprentice to Rainsford Waterhouse of London, merchant, to serve him in Jamaica 5 yeares, the said Mr. Waterhouse haveing paid his debts and discharged him out of prison.   May 22, 1685.
14/260

WHITTELL, Joseph of Redding (Reading),   Berkshire, shearman.   Bound to Philip Gowre for 4 years in Jamaica.   March 6, 1684.   14/170

WHITTINGHAM, Thomas of Rainbury (Wrenbury), Cheshire, gardener. Bound to David Lockwood for 4 years in Jamaica. Nov. 3, 1684.   14/49

WICKHAM, Thomas.   Bound to Robert Shanks for 4 years in Jamaica. Age 28.   Nov. 20, 1684.   Footnote "near the Shipp in Wapping".   14/69

WICKS, Suzanna of Stanwell, Middlesex, spinster.   Bound to Josias Dowell for 4 years in Jamaica.   Oct. 18, 1684.   14/67

WICKS, Thomas.   Bound to William Bennett for 5 years in Virginia. Dec. 9, 1685.   Wintess Jane Copplee, his mother, wife of Samuel Copplee.
14/475

WILBOW or WILLBOW, Jacob.   Son of Eustace Wilbow.   Bound to Robert Burman for 5 years in Maryland.   July 21, 1685.   Witness Ann Guffee of Spitlefeilds (London).   (See also GUFFY, John).   14/333

WILD, Alice, spinster.   Bound to Anthony Gester for 4 years in Virginia. Age 20.   Sept. 21, 1685.   Witness Robert Young of Ratcliffe (London)
14/409

WILKINSON, John.   Bound to Frances Manby (male) for 4 years in Barbados.   June 5, 1683.   13

WILLIAM, Charles.   Son of Charles Williams, late of St. Giles in the Fields, Middlesex.   Bound to Geo. Couch for 4 years in Barbadoes.   Age 14. July 10, 1685.   Consent of his uncle Edward Williams, living in Hampton Towne (probably Middlesex).   14/321

WILLIAMS, Elizabeth.   See Anne SIMONDS.

WILLIAMS, Jane, of Newgate Street, London.   Bound to John Clarke for 4 years in Virginia.   Sept. 16, 1685.   Witness Lyddy Williams, her mother.
14/404

WILLIAMS, Margaret of Tanworth, Warwickshire, spinster.   Bound to Phillipp Clarke for 4 years in Maryland.   July 28, 1684.   13

WILLIAMS, Waller.   Son of John Williams, late citizen and merchant of London.   By consent of Dorothy Williams of Drury Lane, Middlesex, his mother.   Bound to Thomas Hilton of Porte Royall, Jamaica, apothecary, for 7 years.   "The said Hilton by an indorsement on the backside of one of the indentures of apprenticeshipp did covenant and promise not to imploy him in anie other business than what related to the trade of apothecary; therefore by indorsement on the backside of the other indenture, he is not obliged to pay to his said apprentice according to the customs of the country at the expiracion of the said terme".   March 31, 1685.   14/205

WILLIAMS, Walter.   Son of Thomas Williams, Monmouth, husbandman.   Bound to Andrew Perry for 4 years in Jamaica.   Oct. 31, 1684.   14/47

WILLIAMSON, Mary.   Daughter of William Williamson, late of Deptford, Kent, deced.   Bound to Edward Coomes for 4 years in Jamaica.   March 19, 1684.
14/191

WILLINGTON, Mary of London, spinster.   Bound to Sager Walter for 4 years in Jamaica.   Nov. 17, 1684.
14/64

WILLIS, Edmond.   Son of Thomas Willis of Benson, Oxfordshire, farmer, deced.   Bound to Christopher Jefferson for 4 years in St. Christophers.   Feb. 23, 1685.
14/529

WILLOWES, George.   Bound to Philip Clarke for 4 years in Maryland.   July 25, 1684.   13

WILLS, James, citizen and grocer of London.   Bound to Philip Beckett for 4 years in Jamaica.   Age 23.   Jan. 23, 1684.   (See addenda).   14/133

WILSON, Andrew.   Bound to John Williams for 4 years in Virginia.   Age 21.   March 12, 1684.
14/181

WILSON, Elizabeth.   Daughter of John Wilson of London,   joyner.   Bound to Francis Jervis for 5 years in Virginia.   Dec. 31, 1685.   14/488

WILSON, George.   Son of George Wilson, late of Buckson (Buxton?), Norfolk.   Bound to Christopher Squire for 6 years in Jamaica.   Age 19. Nov.. 29, 1684.   14/78

WILSON, John.   Son of John Wilson, late of Hemsley (Helmsley), Yorkshire, deced.   Bound to Robert Shanks for 4 years in Jamaica.   Age 22.   Dec. 1, 1684.   14/82

WINDELL, Henry of London, leather gilder.   Bound to John and Elizabeth Haynes for 4 years in Maryland.   Age 20.   July 6, 1685.   14/317

WINTER, Walter.   Son of William Winter of Wallingford, Berkshire, tallowchandler.   Bound to Gilbert Crouch for 5 years in Maryland.   Age 14. Dec. 2, 1685.   14/467

WINTON, Robert.   Son of Edward Winton, now a prisoner in K. Bench (King's Bench).   Bound to William Marshall for 4 years in Barbadoes. Age 24.   June 16, 1686.   Witness Walter Curidon of Red Lyon Court.   14

WISDOME, Thomas.   Bound to Robert Marshall for 4 years in Barbadoes Nov. 15, 1682.   13

WOOD, Elizabeth.   Bound to Captain Simon Flew for 4 years in Jamaica. Aug. 1, 1683.   13

WOOD, Hannah, spinster.   Bound to Abraham Barrow Lassado for 4 years in Barbadoes.   March 1, 1685.   14/533

WOODBURNE, Mary, daughter of Thomas Woodburne of Southwark, porter. Bound to Anthony Dent for 4 years in Virginia.   Aug. 20, 1685.   Witness Adine Woodburn, her mother.   14/374

WOODHOUSE, Elizabeth, spinster.   Bound to Robert Thorne for 4 years in Virginia.   June 30, 1685.   Witness Mr. Cose, Ratcliffe.   14/305

WOODS, Sarah of London, widow.   Bound to James Parsons for 4 years in Jamaica.   Jan. 20, 1684.   14/129

WOODWARD, Thomas.   Bound to Philip Gower for 4 years in Barbadoes.

Age 26.   April 10, 1685.   14/217

WOOLNOUGH, John.   Son of Thomas Woolnough, late of the City of
Gloucester, deced.   Bound to Thomas Blacke for 5 years in Barbadoes.
Age 15.   March 18, 1684.   Witness Samuel Dobson "the apprentice's late
mother's brother. . . that the apprentice has neither father nor mother
living.   14/190

WOOTTON, Edward.   Son of John Wootton of Savoy in the Strand (London),
bellman.   Bound to Moses Pullborne for 7 years in Virginia. July 21, 1685.
                                                                 14/333

WRIGHT, John.   Son of John Wright of Kings Bench Ally, Southwark
(Surrey), taylor, deced.   Bound to John Heslewood for 8 years in Virginia.
July 24, 1684.   13

WRIGHT, Joseph, of Oxford.   Bound to Charles Jones for 4 years in Jamaica.
Age 24.   April 2, 1686.   Witness, Richard Raines, Waterman, of Shadwell.
(Henry Wheatley under same entry).   14/557

WYATT, John.   Son of Thomas Wyatt of Stoake (?), in Leicester.   Bound
to John Wyatt for 5 years in Barbadoes.   Feb. 29, 1683.   13

Y

YATES, Martha.   Daughter of John Yates of White Lyon Street, St. Giles in the Fields, Middlesex, deced.   Bound to John Pelly for 4 years in Barbadoes.   Age 20.   April 4, 1685.   14/211

YOUNG, Lucq.   See Le JEUN.

ADDENDA

RICHARDS, Elizabeth.   See William RICHARDS.

WALKER, James.   Son of Henry Walker of Halifax, York(shire), deced., weaver.   Bound to Robert Shanks for 4 years in Jamaica.   Age 22.   Dec.1, 1684.   14/83

WILLS, James.   Add: "By consent of his mother living at Plaistow in Essex, his father being dead. "

Add to Index of Places: Aylsham, Norfolk, 72

Great Whitley, (Witley), Worcestershire, 11

APPENDIX I

EXTRACTS FROM THE LORD MAYOR'S WAITING BOOKS REGARDING
SOME PERSONS WHO WERE ILLEGALLY TAKEN ON BOARD EMIGRANT
SHIPS TO BE SOLD AS SERVANTS IN THE PLANTATIONS.

Aug. 25, 1685.

ORDO PARTRIDGE A TRIMM.

In pursuance of an order of the sessions of the yeare held for this city the 24th instant his Lop. upon heareing of the inre. in difference between Arthur Partridge waterman complte of the one pte. agt. Mathew Trimm of Wapping Wall in the Coty. of Mddx. marriner and master of the ship Judah of the other pte. touching the said Trim his transporting of Eliz. Partridge daughter of the sd. Arthur into Virginia in ptes beyond the seas without the consent of her sd. father and is there deteyned as a servt. being of the age of 17 yeares or thereabouts it appeareing to his Lop. that the said Elizabeth Partridge came voluntarily on board the sd ship lyeing at Gravesend whilest the sd Trim was at London and that the said Elizabeth was of no good reputacon his Lop. by submission and consent of both pties doth order that the said Mathew Trimm do pay downe to the sd Arthur Partridge VI li (six pounds) and give security by bond of 100 L (100 pounds) penalty to bring back the said Elizabeth Partridge passage free on or before the 29th of September, 1686 and to pay the said Elizabeth Partridge 5 li (5 pounds) upon their arrive-all in England and if shee dye before her arriveall in England then to pay the sd five pounds to the sd Arthur his exors or assigns on the 30th of September 1686 to which order the said pties have initially consented by subscribing their names hereto and the sd Mr. Trimm hath pd downe to the sd Arthur Partridge the 6 li (six pounds) above mencoed whereof the sd Arthur hereby acknowledgeth the receipt.

> The mark of the above named A. Partridge
> M. Trimm.
> volume 14 page 379-80.

May 31, 1686.

BOSMORE v. LEECH.

Upon his Lops heareing the complte of Anne Bosmore agt Josias Leech commander of the John and Elizabeth now lyeing at the Redhouse (perhaps meaning Rotherhithe) bound for ptes beyond the seas touching Marke Basmore her brother lately spirited aboard the sd ship with designe to be transported beyond the seas who is there deteyned agt his will and the consent of his freinds contrary to law it appeareing to his Lop that the sd Marke was unlawfully gotten on board the sd ship his Lop doth therefore order that the said Josias Leech do forthwith deliver and set at libty the sd Marke Basmore with such clothes and tooles as belong unto him at his perill wheat demanding or taking any allowance for his dyet, all which the said Josias Leech promised should be performed.

volume 14

Dec. 1, 1700.

JAMES PERRISMORE

This day his Lorpp granted out his warrt. for fetching one James Perrismore from a board the ship called the Society bound for Merryland in parts beyond the seas being inveighled on board the same in ord to be transported as appd. to his Lorrp. by Elizabeth Perrismore, his mother.

volume 16.

December 2, 1701.

EDWARD WILSON

This day his Lorpp granted his warrt for the fetching one Edward Wilson who was lately spirited and inveighled by one Cook from on board the Providence, Capt. Martin comander, now lying at anchor near the Redhouse (perhaps Rotherhithe) in the River of Thames bound for Maryland in Virginia.

volume 16.

Abbreviations: Lop or Lorpp...Lordship.
Pte...part
sd...said
pd...paid
complte...complaint

APPENDIX II

ACTS OF THE PRIVY COUNCIL (COLONIAL), December 13, 1682.

Whereas it has bin represented to his Majesty that by reason of the frequent abuses of a lewd sort of People called Spirits in seducing many of his
Majesty's subjects to go on shipboard where they have been seized and
carried by force to his Majesty's Plantations in America, and that many idle
persons who have listed themselves voluntarily to be transported thither, and
have received money upon entering into service for that purpose, have afterwards pretended they were betrayed, and carried away against their wills and
procured their friends to prosecute the merchants who transported them, or
in whose service they are, by Indictments or Information in the Crown office
in his Majesty's Name, which is a great discouragement to them and an
hinderance to the management of the Trade of the said Plantations and Nav-
igation of this Kingdom, and severall merchants and Planters having made
humble applications to his Majesty that he would be graciously pleased to
Direct such methods for their retaining of servants to serve in his Majesty's
Plantations as in his Royall wisedome, He should think meet, wherby his
Majesty may be so satisfied of their fair dealing, as to take of all Prosecutions
against them at his Majesty's sute, and also that the scandall that now lyes
upon them in generall by reason of such evill disposed persons may not remain upon such as shall for the future follow such methods as his Majesty
shall think fit to be pursued.

His Majesty taking into his Royall Consideration the said request, is
graciously pleased to Declare, that such Merchants, Factors, masters of
shipps or other Persons that shall use the method hereafter following in the
hiring of servants for his Majesty's Plantations, shall not be disquieted by any
sute on his Majesty's behalf, but, upon certificate therof, that he will cause
all such sutes to be stopped, to the end they may receive no further Molest-
ation therby:

1. Such servants are to be taken by Indenture to be executed by the
servant in the presence of the Magistrat or Magistrats herafter appointed
one part therof signed by such servant, and also underwritten or endorsed
with the name and handwriting of such Magistrat, which is to remain
with the clerk of the Peace to be returned to the next sessions there to
be filed upon a distinct file, and numbred and kept with the Records.

2. The clerk of the Peace is to keep a fair book, wherin the name of
the Person so bound, and the magistrats name before whom the same was
don, and the time and place of doing therof, and the number of the file

95

shalbe entred, and for the more easy finding the same, the Entries are to be made alphabetically according to the first letter of the surname.

3. All persons above the age of one and twenty yeares or who shall upon view and examination appear to be so in the Judgment of the Magistrate may be bound in the presence of one Justice of the Peace, or of the Mayor or Cheif Magistrate of the place where they shall go on shipboard, who is to be fully satisfied from him of his free and voluntary agreement to enter into the said service.

4. If any person be under the age of one and twenty years, or shall appear so to be, he shalbe bound in the presence of the Lord Mayor of London, or One of the Judges, or an Alderman of London who shall carefully examin whether the person so to be bound have any Parents or Masters, and if he be not free they are not to take such Indenture unlesse the Parents or Masters give their Consent, and some person that knows the said servant to be of the name and addition mentioned in the Indenture is to attest his said knowledge upon the said Indenture.

5. If the person be under the age of fourteen years, unlesse his Parents shall be present and consent, he is not to be carried on shipboard till a fortnight at least after he becomes bound to the intent that if there be any abuse it may be discovered before he be transported. And where his parents do not appear before the Magistrate, notice is to be sent to them, or where they cannot be found to the Church wardens or Overseers of the Parish where he was last setled in such manner as the said Magistrate shall think fit and direct.

And because the Clerks of the Peace may Conceive this not to be any part of the duty of their office, and may therfore exact unreasonable Rewards for their trouble and pains therin, His Majesty doth declare that if any merchants or other Persons shall be aggrieved therby, and upon Complaint to the Justices, cannot obtain relief, his Majesty will take such further Care for their ease herein, as in his Royall wisedome, hee shall think meet.

And his Majesty's further pleasure is, that this order be printed and published, to the end all persons whom it may Concern take notice therof, and govern themselves accordingly.

(On the same day, a scire facias is ordered to be brought against Roger Whitley's patent for registering the covenants of servants going to the plantations, as being found of no use, but rather a prejudice to his Majesty's service).

INDEX OF PLACES

London is omitted from this index since it appears on every page.

INDEX OF AGENTS